Controlling development

The Natural and Built Environment series

Editors: Professor Michael J. Bruton, University of Wales, Cardiff
Professor John Glasson, Oxford Brookes University

Controlling development

Certainty and discretion in Europe, the USA and Hong Kong

Philip Booth
University of Sheffield

UCL
PRESS

First published in 1996 by UCL Press

UCL Press Limited
University College London
Gower Street
London
WC1E 6BT

and

1900 Frost Road, Suite 101
Bristol
Pennsylvania 19007-1598

The name of University College London (UCL) is a registered trade mark used
by UCL Press with the consent of the owner.

British Library Cataloguing in Publication Data
A catalogue record for this book is available from the British Library.

ISBNs: 1-85728-584-0   HB
          1-85728-585-9   PB

Typeset in Times Roman and Optima.
Printed and bound by
Bookcraft (Bath) Ltd, England.

Contents

Preface

The origins of this book go back some 15 years when, faced with the organization of a field trip that included a few days in northern France, I attempted to grapple with the complexities of French planning, so that in turn I could brief my students. And a hard time I had of it. Such French sources as I could find, and the few English sources that then existed, all seemed to be based on assumptions that I did not seem to share. Intrigued, I dug deeper. As I began to absorb the preoccupations of French commentators, two questions in particular formed themselves in my mind. One was to do with the constant reference to certainty in planning that recurred again and again in French texts, and I began to wonder how far the system of planning control in France actually delivered that certainty. The other had to do with the location of real decision-making power, particularly in view of the decentralization of power to local authorities set in train by President Mitterrand from 1982 onwards. I began to see that planning control could not be considered as some kind of objective, independent phenomenon, and that it was in effect a creature of certain understandings about the role of government, the purpose of law and the pattern of administration.

At first I was convinced that to make comparisons between Britain and France would not be helpful and that the best approach was to investigate the French system of development control from within. Shedding as far as possible my Anglo–Saxon prejudices, but nurtured nevertheless in a tradition of case study research that is distinctly un-French, I began to look at development control cases, first in Dijon and then, a year later, in Lyon. This work led eventually to a doctoral thesis. Having completed the thesis I began to see that, although the development control systems of Britain and France could not easily be compared at a superficial level, each nevertheless confronted a similar set of problems. One of those problems had to do with certainty. Another was the question of the discretion offered by the systems to decision-makers to deal with the unforeseen circumstance. And arising from those two was the question of the means by which decision-makers were held to account for the decisions they took. Britain and France placed very different values on the need for certainty and the discretion to act flexibly, but understanding how the two systems confront those difficult issues brought me a little closer to understanding the fundamental problems of controlling urban development. More recently, acquaintance with some other countries' systems of development control, and in particular that of Hong Kong, has helped me to develop my ideas further.

For me, the book represents a stage in an exciting adventure, and like all adventures may well have failed to reach its target. If it does so fail, it will not have been for the want of help. Over the years, friends and colleagues in both Britain and France have pointed me in the right direction and given me much practical assistance.

Ten years ago, Irene Wilson, who was then by far the most knowledgeable person in Britain on the French planning system, gave me the help and encouragement – and the introductions – that got me going. Periods of sabbatical leave were spent at the University of Dijon and at Lyon at the Laboratoire de Géographie Rhodanienne and the Institut d'Urbanisme. I am grateful for the way that Michel Fromont, Jacques Bèthemont and particularly Marc Bonneville, respectively, have facilitated my work. At Lyon, too, Pierre Comte of the University of St Étienne, and more recently Jean-Marc Petit, have been unstinting in providing research material and in putting me right on questions of planning law. Vincent Renard and Joseph Comby of the Association des Études Foncières have given me valuable opportunities to explain the British system to French audiences, a process that in itself has been an important means of deepening my understanding of French perceptions of development control. Members of the French administration have been equally helpful, above all Jean Dellus, then Deputy Director, and his colleagues at the Agence d'Urbanisme de la Communauté Urbaine de Lyon, but also staff at the Communauté Urbaine de Lyon and at the *DDE* of Côte-d'Or, Hérault and Rhône. I am also indebted to the mayors of communes in Rhône, Haute-Loire and Hérault who spent time answering my sometimes impertinent questions.

At home, I have not been short of help either. The ESRC funded some of the French case studies through grants under their Exchange Awards Scheme. John Glasson, Peter Hall, Patsy Healey and Ian Masser offered encouragement and good ideas on the original book proposal. At UCL Press Roger Jones's enthusiasm has been an important stimulus. Pamela Ward read parts of the draft of the book and offered much useful advice. My colleagues at the University of Sheffield covered some of my duties during two periods of sabbatical leave. And Val Heap produced the typescript with despatch and the minimum of fuss.

To all of these, I offer my thanks.

Sheffield, September 1995

CHAPTER 1
Controlling development

Development control, the term used in Britain to define the system of issuing permits for land-use development, has for the most part been a much vilified process. Although the nadir of its fortunes has passed – the low point seems to have been somewhere between 1980 and 1985 – to British ears the term rings with overtones of bureaucratic time-wasting and negativism. From within the planning profession, too, development control has not always been seen in a favourable light. For long the Cinderella of the profession, as several commentators have described it, until the 1980s it tended to attract less well qualified staff and to be associated with drudgery. The smart thing for new recruits to the profession was forward planning, and a stint in development control was regarded as a necessary evil on the path to membership of the Royal Town Planning Institute. Some of that at least has changed; there is nothing now to suggest that development control staff have fewer qualifications than their colleagues who prepare plans, and development control has for some time been recognized as no less intellectually challenging than plan-making. Yet even today, planning literature has rather less to say about the control of development than it does about plan-making and policy.

In general terms, there are several reasons why development control has had such a bad press. One is the fact that the ultimate sanctions in controlling development is to say "no", and it is hardly surprising if, therefore, the whole process is seen as negative. Another is the way in which the public at large find development controllers an easy scapegoat for developments that they dislike: the results of the development control officer's activities are all too enduring. A third is that the reasoning used to justify decisions may appear arcane to outsiders. A fourth – reflecting attitudes within the planning profession – is the degree of separateness, that development control activity traditionally had from the process of making policy. If forward planners with their relatively distant time horizons and large vision could look down on development controllers' petty concerns for back extensions and changes of use, development controllers could consider themselves as under pressure and under-valued.

The extent of vilification to which development control has been subject in Britain over the past 25 years suggests that it may be a rather more important process than its detractors allow. The importance of the process has, at one level, to do with matters of substance. Questions of land-use and urban form affect pro-

1

foundly the welfare and enjoyment of life of those who live in urbanized societies like ours. Decisions taken in the course of development control have a long-term impact. At another level, however, the development control process serves as a focus for a whole range of questions about how we govern ourselves and on whom we confer the power to take decisions on our behalf. Although there are many other areas of the administration of daily life that also raise questions, they become particularly acute in relation to the control of development, because the results of the decisions taken are tangible and enduring.

The struggle to control urban form for reasons of health, aesthetics and social control became a key element in the search for civic identity and local economy in the nineteenth and early twentieth centuries in this country. In France, more recently, urban planning and control have been a major part of the powers that were devolved to local authorities in the decentralization reforms of the early 1980s. The questions are, in other words, not confined to Britain alone, even if the terms in which they are couched here are specific to this country. At yet another level, development control, and the forward planning to which it is related, confront us with an even deeper set of issues about how we deal with the problem of future uncertainty, and contain the fear that uncertainty brings. A study of Britain alone could of itself offer some interesting insights into the way in which these questions are resolved and the problems that solving them then creates. To make comparisons between countries, however, is to widen the debate to reveal the universality of some of these fundamental issues, but also of the very different strategies that have been devised to deal with them.

Yet to make comparisons is to open up another set of difficulties. I have argued elsewhere (Booth 1992) that to compare systems for making plans and controlling development in different countries is to ignore the extent to which both are culturally determined. Plans and development control do not mean the same thing in every country: intentions and expectations differ. If that means comparing the practice in country A with that in country B runs the dangers of being a futile exercise – it is too easy to conclude that systems differ because they are different – at a deeper level the basic problems of systems of development control face are shared. Comparing Britain and France, whose systems are the focus of this book, sheds light on both the difficulties of making comparisons and upon the potential rewards. For all that they share membership of the European Union and are no longer divided by even the 22 miles of the Straits of Dover, and for all that their respective histories have been interlinked, Britain and France have a radically different understanding of the nature of the state, of the nature and purpose of administration, and by extension of the way development control should be practised. The way the two countries cope with certainty and uncertainty; the way they allow for and resist freedom of manoeuvre in decision-making, the way that they make their systems accountable, are in the final analysis important in probing the central dilemmas that all systems face.

Supplementing British and French experience with that of other countries is intended to show the extent to which fundamental problems are shared and are not unique to Britain and France, and to cast a sharper focus on certain issues that are less well exposed in Britain and France. The purpose of this book is specifically to explore some of those questions.

The purposes of development control

Within the framework of the British Town and Country Planning Acts, development control is the mechanism by which the policies contained in development plans can be implemented. To describe British development control in this way is to obscure the nature of both its origins and its present practice. Elsewhere, this kind of link is, in any case, viewed in rather different terms. What becomes increasingly clear, in looking at other systems as well as that of Britain, is that everywhere controlling development by regulating building form precedes the process of making plans. Only in this century has the issuing of permits really been bolted on to a system of plan-making, and with it the idea that development control has an explicitly strategic role in implementing policy, as well as being a tactical response to development pressure in the hope of limiting abuses. But even in its most mindless regulatory mode and in the absence of plans, the control of development has also expressed some kind of strategic vision. Indeed, control has served, and serves still, several quite distinct ends, all of which imply a strategy of some kind.

The first has to do with the search for the image of the ideal city. Although concern for perfect city form is as old as cities themselves, the idea that the form of a city could express the ideal order for society in its regularity and its harmony gathered a new momentum in the Renaissance. More importantly, it was the Renaissance rulers of Europe who began to develop the administrative means to ensure that vision could become a reality. The story traced in Chapters 2 and 3 begins with the attempts by Henri IV in France and the Stuart kings of England to control new building by intervening in the development process. In London in particular, from the beginning of the seventeenth century, there was an attempt to impose an image of unity and order by incremental decisions made about individual proposals for development. If Henri IV and Charles I were motivated by a desire to create static and harmonious cities at the very moment when urban life and society were acquiring a new and disturbing dynamism, the concern for aesthetics and appropriate appearance did not die with them. Concern for the well ordered city, the city beautiful, continues to be an important spur to controlling development.

The second purpose that is identifiable from the same period is apparently of a very different order. Elizabeth I had already in the late sixteenth century sought to limit new buildings on new foundations as a way of controlling the influx of migrants that appeared to threaten social order. In Paris, too, the same kind of limitation was imposed. Under the Stuarts, the outright interdiction was replaced

3

with something rather different: a filtering process whereby the gentry and aristocracy were if anything encouraged to come to London. Only the poor were to be excluded. In fact this approach to social control was more closely linked to the visual perfection of the city than might at first appear. A sanitized aesthetic was part of a vision of the ideal city that had no place for civil unrest that the poor would be likely to bring in their wake. Development control to achieve social control, still sometimes disguised as control over aesthetics, remains an issue in the twentieth century. Exclusionary zoning, to keep out undesirables, remains a key to the debate on zoning ordinances in the USA, and the undertow of concern for social exclusivity has informed development control decisions in Europe, too.

The third purpose of development control was the control of disease and the promotion of good health. Here an apparently humanitarian motive for controlling development has been linked to a fear of social disorder that disease seems to threaten. However it may be, the introduction of regulations in this country to control the form and layout of new housing was a major factor in improving housing conditions and the health of the city has a whole, even if regulatory control had the effect of driving up prices and excluding the very poor from the better housing conditions that were being created. Nevertheless, the outbreaks of cholera and typhoid of the first half of the nineteenth century had by the end of the century become a thing of the past. Moreover, regulations that were based on the theory that disease was airborne resulted in a hitherto unknown spaciousness in working-class housing.

With the fourth purpose of development control comes a new dimension. The first three purposes imply a role for controlling development that is essentially reactive: once the decision to develop has been taken, then public authorities intervene to ensure that the aesthetic, social or sanitary concerns are met. Clearly, all these concerns do have a strategic element, to make the city more harmonious, socially cohesive, or healthy, by restricting the activities of individuals. But they could only be described in the loosest sense as representing spatial strategies. The idea that it might be desirable to intervene before the decision to develop has been taken, emerges only in the second half of the nineteenth century, with moves in Europe and the USA to develop a system of land-use plans. On to these plans were then attached the older systems of regulatory control that now became informed by a new purpose, to ensure that new development complied with the long-term vision for the way in which urban areas were developed. For the first time, public authorities began to be concerned not only with controlling the physical form of development, but also with the use to which land would be put, independent of the form. The possibility of development control as an activity to promote development in accordance with a strategy rather than just to regulate it, was now in place.

A final purpose that development control has come to serve, at least in this country, is of a quite different order. Because of the wide-ranging factors that may now be taken into account in determining planning applications, development control has also became a way of resolving conflicts. In theory, neighbour disputes are no concern of the public authority acting in the public interest. In practice, defining the boundary between general public welfare and the narrow concerns of neighbours is not very easy. Sometimes a neighbour dispute is based upon matters of wider concern. Sometimes a general policy when applied to a particular case is relevant only to those immediately affected. Either way, the development control process has become a useful means of balancing conflicting interests, and such interests may well transcend those of neighbours in dispute or owners concerned with property values. As the sense of individual rights and freedoms has grown, so too has the need for development control to assume the function of resolver of conflicts. This has also had the effect of making development control mechanisms pig in the middle, excoriated by developers for failing to take their interests seriously and exposing them to unnecessary risks, and loathed by community and environmental interests for failing to be sufficiently robust in their response to developers.

Regulatory and discretionary control

So, development control serves several different purposes and, although it is now used as a means of implementing land-use plans, it pre-dates them. However, there is also a question about the nature of the control exercised. Although at the outset attempts at controlling development everywhere appear to have followed the pattern of establishing regulatory norms in the form of measurable dimensions, by the twentieth century, when controlling development was linked to a newly emerging system of land-use plans, two distinct families of development control system had emerged, which can be described respectively as discretionary and regulatory. The fact that there are two such families of development control does not have to do with different understandings of the nature of urban growth and development. On the other hand, it has everything to do, with different understandings of the role of law, proper administration and the nature of regulation.

Discretionary systems of development control are those like Britain's, and the systems in the English-speaking world that have adopted British practice. They are built on a tradition of case law and of a pragmatism that has been suspicious of attempts to identify the full scope of action in advance, in the belief that it is impossible to predict all the circumstances that may obtain in advance of a decision on a particular planning application. In discretionary systems, therefore, there is no absolute relationship between the plan and the development control decisions, which in the event may depend on other factors than the plan. Plans are thus indicative of policy, but not definitive. Moreover, development control can exist in the absence of formal plans, yet still invoke criteria based on putative planning policy. Discretionary systems are praised for their flexibility, but create potentially difficult problems about the relationship of the decisions on planning applications to the policy contained in plans. They may lead to a kind of para-

5

policy – that is to say, policy that is implicit in the accumulation of individual decisions but is not evident in formal policy documents. They imply a high level of trust in the decision-makers, who may be politicians. There is a notable absence of certainty in such systems.

Regulatory systems derived from countries that have developed administrative law or that have a written constitution that defines rights and privileges. In such systems, planning control has to be clear in defining the rights of individuals as landowners and the precise limits to those rights. Most of the European Union countries apart from England and Ireland have systems of planning control of this kind. So, too, does the USA. Development control has, therefore, to be based on a complete statement of what is permissible made in advance: in theory at least, nothing can be left until the moment at which the decision is taken. From this there are several consequences. The decisions on planning applications have rather less significance than is the case in discretionary systems, because in principle they are no more than a confirmation that the proposed development conforms to the regulations in the plan. By contrast the plan is of considerable significance because it contains all the criteria against which an application can be judged. A clear definition of rights also gives rise to the possibility of challenge and to the right of redress. On the other hand, controlling development becomes in principle more difficult in the absence of a plan. Great premium is placed upon certainty: the certainty of knowing in advance what is acceptable and the certainty of obtaining a favourable decision if all the regulations are met.

Within regulatory systems of control, two distinct types of system are discernible. There are those like France's in which the systems of plans identify both short- and long-term policy, but at the same time offer a precise definition of zones with regulations attaching to them. In such systems there is a continuum from strategic policies to the eventual decision on a particular development proposal for a given plot. On the other hand, the US system proposes a clear distinction between plans that offer long-term policy and zoning ordinances that identify zones and articulate detailed regulations. In principle in the USA, zoning ordinances are prepared in the light of policy in a plan, but since many municipalities have no plan, zoning ordinances in most cases stand alone as the sole form of policy that applies. In the French case, that kind of tension between regulatory control and forward planning is in principle avoided by the use of a single document to cover both. In practice there is the suspicion that local plans in France are forced to serve two not always compatible ends: to identify existing rights and so frame a *status quo,* and to present a programme for future change.

Any system of planning or development control, whether it is essentially discretionary or regulatory, is confronted with the problem of how the criteria on which control decisions are based are to be expressed. Of course, there are differences in emphasis. Regulatory systems, predicated on the desire for certainty and the need to define rights, has favoured rules that offer measurable limits to the development acceptable in any given plot. Discretionary systems, where they do have explicit criteria, have preferred to maintain their flexibility by the use of open-ended wording, often qualified by words such as "normally". However, both approaches have their limitations. The fixed limits may provide a rigidity that is neither desired nor desirable; the open-ended policy exhortation may leave the decision-maker and the applicant bereft of appropriate courses of action in particular cases. However, the examination of the purposes development control is designed to serve suggests that the argument is not simply one of rules versus open-ended criteria. Some objectives may well find their appropriate expression in fixed limits. Others may need to take the form of standards to be attained or performance criteria against which a purpose may be evaluated. Knowing what kind of expression is appropriate to what kind of problem is fundamental to finding a successful policy base for development control decisions. Confronting the difficulties that certain kinds of expression pose for the system of control is equally vital to the process.

A final issue to be considered is that of the mechanisms that exist for taking decisions. Here the pattern is immensely varied, but a general distinction is worth observing between administrative and political channels for decision-making. In practice, much *de facto* decision-making, even if it is not directly sanctioned by statute, is undertaken by technical services of one kind or another, who see their competence as either administrative or more narrowly focused, as professional. In either case the competence is couched in terms of expertise gained through training and involving allegiance to a particular ethos. Political decision-making, on the other hand, is about taking decisions to reflect the interests of a clientele or an electorate. In very general terms, regulatory systems stress administrative decision-making; discretionary systems, political. In fact the distinction between systems and between types of decision-making is anything but clear cut. From the 1960s, community groups and others began to accuse professionals of being political in their decision-making and in both regulatory and discretionary systems it is possible to find a heady mix of political and professional judgement and complicated relationships between politicians, professionals and administrators. Who takes decisions and how are questions of some significance in considering development control.

Public action and private interest

Both the purpose that controlling development has acquired, and the systems for development control that have been described in the previous section, give rise to some more basic questions to do with the control of land and the nature of government. Central to this debate is the relationship between landownership and control by public authorities. Modern systems of controlling development have arisen as a direct result of the growth of private landownership and the consequent readjustment of the role of government. In theory at least, in feudal Europe the monarch's land was his to dispose of as he would; anyone else's rights

7

to use land were strictly conditional on the monarch's will. The eventual weakening of feudalism and the gradual development of a market in land in which in Britain the Crown became heavily implicated after the Reformation also led to an inexorable weakening of the traditional means by which the Crown controlled its subjects. Although direct intervention was still possible, and the Stuarts had ambitious plans for their capital, which lack of finance made it difficult to complete, the attempts at regulation after 1600 were a direct reflection of a new relationship between the state and the individual.

Thereafter, the problem that confronted public authorities was to determine precisely what their role should be. Should they intervene directly to secure development objectives? Should they exercise a regulatory control to prevent the worst excesses of individuals acting on their own initiative? Should they in fact take no action, and rely on self-interest to secure the desired end? In Britain, with a highly sophisticated private market in land, there was, from the middle of the seventeenth century to the middle of the nineteenth century, remarkably little desire – or for that matter capacity – on the part of government to take direct action or even to impose strict regulatory control. In France, by contrast, with a far more sophisticated administration, direct intervention and close regulation, although applied somewhat fitfully, was nevertheless the order of the day well before the industrial revolution. The debate remains current.

There was another kind of tension in the role that government could take in controlling development. This was between that of the impartial authority acting for the greater good – of the kingdom, the people, the state, it did not matter very much which – and that of an institution also heavily implicated in the development process for its own ends. The Stuarts' desire to control development appears to have arisen from the desire to sell licences. Two centuries later, the Prince Regent, with grandiose ambitions for London's West End, nevertheless promoted development in a way that compared directly with that of the other aristocratic landlords who were instrumental in changing London. The Crown Estate became first among equals of great landlords, with a vast financial stake in the development of the West End.

The modern form of this tension is seen most clearly in the case of Hong Kong (examined in Ch. 4), where government is virtually the only landlord. But within the general tension, between government acting as impartial judge of the public good and government standing to make direct gain from developments, are two separate issues. One has to do with the mechanism of control. Here the problem is whether the agreement between the landlord and the lessee, or the contract between the purchaser and vendor, both of which may be subject to restrictive covenants, does in fact ensure that the purposes of development control can be met. The other has to do with the benefits that may accrue to government itself from controlling the use of land. Although the benefits may indeed be direct financial gain through the sale of lease premiums or from rental income, the twentieth century has seen the development of negotiated agreements, which provide benefits in cash or in kind to satisfy other policy objectives of the controlling authority. These agreements, although taking various forms, are widely used. They are in evidence in both Britain and France, and in both countries have been the subject of considerable concern because of the fear that local authorities may become too greedy and exert undue leverage on developers in the hope of gain. Whether or not the fear is well founded, the search for material interest in the control process turns the controlling authority from impartial adjudicator into an equal partner with the developer. This in turn has consequences for the controlling authority's relationship with other interests with a stake in the outcome of a control decision. Yet again, maybe the very idea of government as an impartial adjudicator acting in the public interest is an inherently false model of the nature of the development control process. Perhaps the explicit recognition of mutual interest in agreements gives a truer picture of the nature of development control.

Certainty, flexibility and accountability

Under these questions of relationships, there is yet another layer of concern about the way in which controlling authorities behave towards those they control and the public at large. Here there are three themes that recur in all the systems discussed in this book and which create problems for all systems of planning control. First, all systems for controlling development are designed to cope with the problem of future uncertainty. The Stuart monarchs controlled development to reduce the unpredictability of social unrest and to lessen the visual disorder of the medieval city. So, too, in the nineteenth century, regulations tried to stem the threat of the outbreak of disease and ensure higher standards of public health. More recently, development control has also been about ensuring that policy and plans could be implemented as individual development decisions are taken. Development control, with its potentially wide remit, also therefore takes on one of the oldest fears: that of the unknowable future with its potential for disaster.

The guarantees that systems for controlling development offer are not just to the government, however. Developers look for certainty to guide their decisions and to lessen their risk, while the general public sees in the control of development a means whereby their collective and individual interests may be protected. The certainty that a view will remain intact, that land values will not be eroded, that a loved or fragile environment will not come to harm – are all potentially important. A very great deal is, therefore, posited in what is sometimes categorized as being just a boring administrative chore. However, the question for public authorities is how to ensure that they can deliver a degree of certainty that the users of the system require. Hence, the ever more elaborate rules for how decisions should be taken; hence, too, the use of land-use plans to ensure certainty in the spatial distribution of activities and building form. But in every case the problem does not arise when development proposals conform more or less to expectations. The real problem is where the proposal is unexpected and does not conform. Then systems of control are always tested and the certainties that the systems are designed to promote are threatened with extinction.

The second theme has to do with flexibility and discretion. If coping with uncertainty and the problem of creating certainty form one kind of test for development control, another has to do with the responsiveness to unforeseen circumstances. One of the things that becomes clear in looking at any system of controlling development is that a desire to create certainty is matched by an equal and opposite tendency to look for flexibility in the taking of decisions. This desire, by no means confined to discretionary systems of control alone, is often expressed in terms of coping with uncertainty. We cannot be sure in advance, the argument goes, of what development will be needed where, or indeed when it will be needed. We need to reflect that uncertainty by retaining the margin of manoeuvre for the moment when a decision must be taken. Legitimate though these arguments may be, they also are bound up with a different question, that of discretion. And in talking about discretion, the argument begins to turn to the issue of who takes decisions and with what authority. It shifts the focus away from substance of the decision to the manner in which it is taken.

The third theme is that of accountability. Whenever there is discretion to act – and as we shall see, that is very frequent in practice – the question of how, if at all, the decision-makers can be held to account follows inevitably. Systems based on a tradition of administrative law tend to see the prime means of accountability as being through judicial process. Discretionary systems have preferred to emphasize administrative procedures to ensure accountability. But, as elsewhere, this simplistic distinction obscures the fact that all systems of development control offer a variety of forms of accountability and, by extension, of redress for those aggrieved by the decisions taken. Moreover, the tests used to make decision-makers accountable also vary. Thus, in administrative law systems, legality may still be the criterion applied, even where the procedure is administrative not legal. Nor is the concept of legality absent merely because a system of control relies on administrative and political means for ensuring that decision-makers account for their actions.

The chapters that follow attempt to present the forces that have shaped the control of development in Britain and France, and the effects, for better or worse, of the systems that the two countries have created. The first part of the book is, therefore, descriptive, and it presents the contrasting character of the two systems and the way they have evolved. To that has been added a series of limited sketches of other systems, partly in order to highlight the particular tensions that are present in a more muted form in Britain and France, and partly to demonstrate that particular issues are not unique to those two countries. The second part of the book takes up the three key themes of certainty, flexibility and discretion, and accountability, which have been outlined above. Here the emphasis is on process rather than substance; but, to bring the process to life, the thematic chapters draw extensively on case studies. The book concludes with an evaluation of the two systems and an attempt to lay down markers for the future of development control.

CHAPTER 2
Britain

The British development control system is in many ways a curious creature. The 1947 Town and Country Planning Act that gave birth to the system in its current form, provided for both a hierarchy of plans and a method of overseeing individual development decisions that was loosely based on the policy that the plans presented. However, there was no guarantee of rights to develop nor any certainty that permission would be forthcoming if applied for. Moreover, the whole concept of control was defined to include not only buildings, but also changes of use, even if no construction work was involved. Wide-ranging control, absence of any certainty for landowners and developers, and considerable leeway accorded to development control decision-makers, are the hallmarks of the British system. In all these characteristics, it stands apart from the systems of most of its European partners. However, the system does embrace a variety of different ends, which, if not necessarily in conflict, at least has a very varied impact on the way the system works. The origins of this bundle of contradictions, tensions and diverging objectives, subsumed into a single administrative process, require exploration.

The origins of the British development control system

Although there were certainly attempts to control both land use and construction during the Middle Ages, it is not until the end of the Tudor monarchy that we begin to find concerted attempts to control development that were to pave the way for the modern system. During the sixteenth century, London was beginning its relentless growth that by the eighteenth century was to make it the largest city in Europe, if not in the world. For Queen Elizabeth I, the growth was, it would appear, profoundly disturbing: the image of a city in the constant process of expansion was at odds with the traditional vision of society that was hierarchical and static. Moreover, the influx of a population that was rootless and destitute was the source of a more immediate danger of social unrest. From 1580 onwards, royal proclamations forbade the building of houses on new foundations, and what had been started by Elizabeth I was repeated by her Stuart successors. It was an early attempt to use control of physical development to achieve social control

11

and maintain social stability, which was applied through an Act of 1589, not only to London, but to the country as a whole (Knowles & Pitt 1972). All that can be said of these decrees, as of the Act itself, is that they were spectacularly unsuccessful in achieving their end: population and coverage of land by buildings continued to increase. The experience was an early lesson in the problems of policy implementation: that no system of control can be effective without adequate enforcement.

Aesthetic and social control under the Stuart monarchy

With the Stuarts, however, came an important shift of emphasis. An Ordinance of 1607 already makes reference to the need to "adorn and beautify" the city when rebuilding took place on old foundations. By 1615 James I was expressing the desire that he should be remembered for having "found Our Citie and Suburbs of London of Sticks and left them of Bricks being a Meteriall farre more durable, safe from Fire, beautiful and magnificent" (edict of 1618, cited by Knowles & Pitt 1972: 19). That was followed in 1619 by a proclamation that for the first time began to lay down norms for building construction. This desire for embellishment stemmed from an increased awareness of the architecture of the Italian renaissance, which was very largely promoted by the informed knowledge of Inigo Jones and his aristocratic patrons (Summerson 1953, Harris 1989). As Summerson puts it, "Taste in architecture reached London about 1615 . . ." (Summerson 1947: 11). The desire to recreate London in a more noble guise did not merely find expression in royal proclamations. In 1618, James I set up a Commission on Buildings, for which Inigo Jones, as Surveyor to the King's Works, became executive officer. Its function was to propose suitable architectural treatment for new buildings in and around London. The one notable success of the Commission in the period before the Civil War was the control that was exercised on both the layout and design for Covent Garden, from 1630. The story of Covent Garden presents a major departure of what we might now term control by the public sector of private sector development.

The general outline of the Covent Garden story is well enough known (Summerson 1947, 1970, Thorne 1980). The Earl of Bedford, having allowed building to take place on land in his ownership in defiance of royal decrees, applied for a licence to develop what remained of unbuilt land between frontages on Long Acre and Bedford House, fronting the Strand. Charles I agreed to grant such a licence on payment of a fine and on condition that the land was laid out and developed in accordance with designs by the Surveyor General to the Commission. The design that emerged was for housing grouped around a piazza, with its focal point a church at the western end. Complete symmetry about the east–west axis was impossible because of the existence of Bedford House, which precluded a southern range of buildings to match that on the north side. However, in both its regularity and its architectural detail, Covent Garden was revolutionary. Architectural authorship of the design has been the subject of some controversy, but although there is no doubt that Jones designed the Tuscan Doric St Paul's church, the likelihood is that a French architect, Isaac de Caus, working at the court of Charles I, was responsible for the design as well the execution of the houses. Certainly, the façade treatment of the houses, with pilasters in stone applied to brickwork raised over a ground-floor arcade, bear a close resemblance to the surviving buildings in the Place des Vosges, Paris, built in 1604 (Summerson 1953, Thorne 1980, Harris 1989).

The architectural sources and the responsibility for the design are of less significance for present purposes than the process of control itself. Given the royal decrees that continued to forbid new buildings, the fact that any building was permitted at Covent Garden is perhaps surprising. In part, of course, the reasons were entirely venal: the Stuart monarchy saw the levying of fines as a useful source of revenue for the rapidly depleting royal exchequer. As for the explicit desire to achieve the embellishment of the capital through the exercise of control, it is tempting to see more than just a play of higher sensitivities. The desire to make London fair competition for Henry IV and Louis XIII's Paris was perhaps one motive, and the fact that Queen Henrietta Maria was French was no doubt a factor in the emulation. Perhaps, too, the order and regularity of Renaissance architecture began to have an appeal, because they reflected the ideal image of a society that was ordered and hierarchical.

In addition, the desire to make this particular corner of London's western suburb a worthy part of Charles's capital, the Commission did appear to have strategic as well as tactical objectives. Although there was no overall blueprint or plan to be implemented, there clearly was the expectation that the face of London could be made to conform to the new canons of taste by the control of incremental change. Hence, in addition to Covent Garden, there are examples of building in Lincolns Inn Field and Great Queen Street in which the Commission intervened (Survey of London 1912, Summerson 1966). The other aspect of strategic control was social. Documentary evidence makes it clear that Covent Garden was acceptable because it was designed for a well-to-do clientele who would not threaten the established order. Control of building form was thus a means to an exclusionary end.

Elsewhere I have argued that the dramatic change that took place in the form and layout of London's housing in the seventeenth century cannot be ascribed simply to change in taste or the introduction of public control, and that the key determinants of the change were essentially economic (Booth 1980). The increasing tendency to view land and housing as a commodity created its own rationale, but tended to favour a certain kind of building.

Yet in London at least there was public control, which, after the modest achievements of Charles I's Commission, became increasingly sophisticated. The next key event comes after the Restoration with the Great Fire, and the urgent need to rebuild the City's commercial core. Immediately after the fire had been brought under control, first Wren and then Evelyn produced blueprints for an entirely new street plan that employed the baroque vista as the main ordering concept. What happened in practice was very different. Perhaps recognizing how difficult and possibly counterproductive imposing an entirely new plan on the ruins of the City would be, the Commission for Rebuilding, of which Wren and Evelyn were both members, proposed legislation to control rebuilding on existing frontages, with only modest, tactical improvements to street layout.

The Act, passed in 1667, controlled construction details of buildings, including use of materials and required the heights of buildings to be related to the street width. Streets were grouped in four categories. Summerson argues that the controls were not so much innovative as an expression of current best practice (1947) and that the constructional detail was to set a standard for brick building throughout the country (1953). However it may be, the Act provided a control that did not entail direct intervention in the design of the kind exercised by the Commission on Buildings before the Civil War had done, but simply imposed constraints – albeit stringent – on what private builders might do. Within those limits, builders sought an originality in their choice of detail that was denied them in the overall form of the building. Where Charles I's Commission had dealt with development project by project, the Rebuilding Act of 1667 provided a generalized regulatory framework that was reactive and tactical rather than strategic.

The London Building Acts and leasehold control

What the Rebuilding Act did for the destroyed parts of the City, the London Building Act, came to do for new building on greenfield sites in the London suburbs. By the time the first of these acts was passed in 1704, the constructional detailing that was required was well established practice, although the requirement to minimize joinery on the facade did modify the appearance of London's houses. Once again there was no attempt to impose layouts or direct where building was to take place, merely to provide a framework for evaluating proposals, by setting standards that new development needed to achieve. Again, use of materials, thickness of walls and height of buildings in relation to street width were the main features of control. Interestingly, there appears to have been little in the way of an effective administration for enforcing these Acts. In the City, the control was in the hands of the aldermen, who in the Middle Ages had been assisted by City Viewers, a post that appears to have fallen out of use by the eighteenth century. Elsewhere, Justices of the Peace were responsible for the control and they relied on informers (Knowles & Pitt 1972).

The 1774 Building Act represented a further advance: under the Act the size of buildings and their constructional detail was related to their rateable value. Thereafter, a succession of building manuals showed builders the appropriate form of detailing of housing design for the four rates. The Act also allowed for the appointment for surveyors to enforce its provisions. It was to remain in force for over 80 years. The principal weaknesses of the Act were twofold. First, it applied only to City of Westminster and the parishes of St Pancras, St Marylebone and St Luke's Chelsea. Secondly, it no longer required building heights to be related to street widths. A potentially important measure of planning, as opposed to building, control had been lost at the very moment when urban expansion was becoming increasingly rapid.

The fact that the London Building Acts were very largely put into effect is not to be ascribed to the effectiveness of public control. The activities of the private landlord were paramount. Aristocratic landlords became increasingly adept at drawing up contracts and controlling the work of builders to whom they offered leases. The constructional detail of the Acts provided both standards that could ensure that the value of the land was enhanced and an easy way of evaluating results.

By the beginning of the nineteenth century, opinion was deeply entrenched that the provision of land for development and the building of housing was essentially a private sector activity. The doubts that began to set in were a consequence in the end of industrialization. A realization of the scale of the squalor in which people lived in the growing cities of the provinces, an awakening social conscience and fear of disease and of civil unrest – all began to give rise to questions about whether leasehold control was adequate to stem the growth of slums. Much of the debate had to do with the rack-renting that led to the overcrowding of the more dilapidated buildings. The initial remedies were to control overcrowding or to permit local authorities to demolish and to replace unfit housing, although authorities also acted as if the problem would disappear if the buildings were demolished (Wohl 1977, Burnett 1986). Another strand of thinking was to stem the production of new slums. In particular, the desire to outlaw the back-to-back, whose lack of through ventilation was seen as a major evil, led eventually to the introduction of controls (Burnett 1986). However, none of this amounted to planning control.

Public health legislation

The legislation that produced the most dramatic shift was the Public Health Act of 1875. Not the first public health Act to be passed, and not solely concerned with the control of new housing, it nevertheless made important provision for local authorities to control, through by-laws, the way in which housing was constructed and laid out. The Act itself was followed in 1877 by the production of Model By-laws, which local authorities were urged to adopt and most major cities did. An exception was Leeds, which continued to authorize back-to-backs until the 1920s. As Harper (1985) has pointed out, the 1875 Act and the Model By-laws were in fact very largely based on previous legislation. In particular, Model By-laws produced under the Local Government Act 1856, themselves based on the first building legislation for London since the 1774 Act, had set a precedent for nationally produced standards for housing construction and layout.

15

The crucial difference is that, whereas the 1858 by-laws had only limited application, the Model By-laws, for all that they were permissive, were very widely adopted from the 1880s onwards.

Like the London Building Acts of the previous century, the Model By-laws were mainly about providing standards for construction and the internal dimensions of houses, but they also specified minimum dimensions for street width and space between buildings at the rear. They also required that every street had an opening at either end, thus preventing the creation of courts, where some of the worst housing conditions had existed. The effect was to raise substantially the quality of new housing, but to ensure simultaneously that its cost was beyond the reach of poorest strata of society.

However, the Act did reinforce three very important aspects of the control of new development. First, that such control was the proper function of local authorities. Secondly, that such control was primarily to be about the disposition and layout of buildings and to be couched in terms of quantifiable limits. Thirdly, that control was not over location but over form and layout, once location had been determined by the private sector. Control was thus essentially reactive, local and simple to apply. The 1875 Public Health Act did not require local authorities to take action, nor were they obliged to adopt the Model By-laws of 1877. By this stage, however, most major urban authorities had long since been convinced of the necessity for some form of control.

The early planning legislation

The earliest town planning legislation to bear the name, the 1909 Housing, Town Planning, etc. Act, is both a direct descendant of the nineteenth-century attempts to control housing and a reaction to it. Part of the Act was devoted to the provision of housing and to extending the powers under the 1890 Housing of the Working Classes Act, which had allowed local authorities to build housing on new sites without necessarily having demolished slums first. The other part of the Act allowed, although it did not require, local authorities to prepare planning schemes for land that was in the course of development or on which development was expected. Within such schemes, regulations could be imposed, which could be a substitute for existing by-laws under the Public Health Act. In one sense this kind of control is in a direct line of succession to the earlier public health controls, albeit tailored to cope with local problems (Minett 1974). In another, the process of control to be exercised in planning schemes was to prevent the monotony created by by-law streets of the late nineteenth century. Therefore, at least part of the aim was embellishment, not just sanitary control (Punter 1986). Essentially the 1909 Act proposed a zoning system. Control over location could be exercised only within the context of a planning scheme, and, provided that development respected the locational and regulatory requirements of the scheme, it could not in principle be refused. Yet even under the 1909 Act, dimensional regulatory control was giving way to an approach that was essentially discretionary. In the largest scheme to be prepared under the 1909 Act, that for Ruislip–Northwood, the regulations contained the following clause:

> . . . if . . . the Council are of the opinion that the character of the building or buildings to be erected or altered would be injurious to the amenity of the neighbourhood, whether on account of the design or the undue repetition of the design or the materials to be used, the Council may require such reasonable alteration to be made in respect to design or materials as they think fit. (Aldridge 1915, cited by Punter 1986: 352)

Two phrases are striking in this clause. The first is the reference to the undefined concept of amenity, which had made its first appearance in the 1909 Act (Davey & Minshull 1923). The second is the power that the council took upon itself to require alterations as they thought fit. This is a very different order of requirement from a simple dimensional norm and it suggests a growing sophistication both in local administration and in the understanding of the way in which control could be used.

There was of course a larger purpose at work in the 1909 Act, which went beyond the need for tactical control of new buildings, whether that control was regulatory or discretionary. The desire to be able to exercise a strategic control over the pattern of development had been the inspiration for the Act in the first place. In part, it was Ebenezer Howard's work on garden cities, with its proposal for a radical break with existing settlement patterns, which reinforced the view that simply tackling the worst of the sanitary problems was not enough. The direct inspiration, however, was from Germany, where, as early as the 1820s, legislation had permitted local authorities to create planned town extensions to reduce overcrowding and to encourage development (Sutcliffe 1981). A final aspect of the control introduced by the 1909 Act has to do with the relationship between central and local government. The then recently constituted Local Government Board was given the role of approving town planning schemes, which had to be laid before Parliament for 30 days before becoming operational. The Board also became the body to whom landowners and developers could appeal. The increasing freedom to act offered by the law was being offset by increasing surveillance at central government level.

The 1909 Act is generally regarded as ineffective legislation that disappointed its promoters (Cherry 1975, Sutcliffe 1981). Only 13 planning schemes were produced under the legislation and Birmingham accounted for five of them. The 1919 Housing, Town Planning etc. Act was to make good some of the deficiencies. In housing it unleashed the wave of inter-war council house building by making it a duty of local authorities to assess and provide for their housing need, and for the first time providing central government finance to assist local authorities in their task. For town planning schemes, the Act made two important changes. First, the preparation of schemes became obligatory for districts with a population of more than 20 000. Secondly, the need for approval by the Local Government Board was removed, thereby eliminating an important bureaucratic impediment to plan-making. The 1919 Act was therefore seen in comparison with its predecessor as "strong" legislation, and certainly it resulted in a vastly increased planning activity. By 1933, 94 approved schemes and no fewer than 1235 schemes for which at least a resolution to proceed had been prepared (Cherry 1975).

An interesting aspect of the 1919 Act, which is not usually referred to, is the possibility offered, under Section 45, for local authorities to permit development to proceed, pending the preparation of a plan. This overcame the inconvenience of the 1909 Act, which had effectively required a halt on all developments until a plan was approved. The section was given administrative effect by Order:

> For the purposes of Section 45 of the Housing, Town Planning etc. Act 1919, the local authority may permit the development of estates and building operations to proceed in the area, pending preparation and approval of a Town Planning Scheme subject to the conditions contained in this Order. (Town Planning (Interim Development) Order 1922: para. 3).

Paragraph 5 of the Order allowed local authorities to require development to comply with "such requirements as the local authority may reasonably impose". The 1919 Act thus sees the emergence of the practice of control not related to regulatory norms and only partially related to plan preparation, with the explicit recognition that local authorities could act freely, provided it was within reason. The move away from regulatory towards discretionary development control had begun.

As was to become characteristic of development control, wide freedom to act was set about with constraints imposed by government Circular. The purpose of this interim control of development was not to prevent development, but to allow it to proceed:

> The Minister considers it of the greatest importance that private development should not be arrested while a town planning scheme is in course of preparation and that owners should be able to proceed with genuine building plans without fear of the subsequent effects of the scheme . . . The Minister considers that the presumption be always in favour of the person who wishes to undertake development. (Ministry of Health Memoranda, cited by Davey & Minshull 1923: 14, 187)

More important still, the local authorities' requirements were to be "as few and simple as possible". It was as if the government thought that the children might, after all, behave badly with their new found freedom. Planning was still limited to land that was in the course of development or ripe for development, and the control exercised was only over estates and building operations. Both planning schemes and interim control were thus constrained by the nature of the Act.

The 1932 Act and interim development control

The 1932 Town and Country Planning Act was to provide the next step forwards. Its very title gives some clue to the way in which it marked a departure: for the first time unbuilt land could be included in a scheme, even if it was not required for development, and at the same time fully developed land could also be included. Thus, the Act vastly increased the scope of planning control. The second major innovation of the Act was to extend the definition of development, to include not only "Building or rebuilding operations" but also "Any use of the land or the buildings thereon for a purpose, which is different from the purpose for which the land or building was last being used " (§53). Interim development control was thus possible not only over any part of the country if a resolution to produce a scheme had been passed; it also covered land-use as well as building. It allowed a local authority to take a strategic view of the grouping of buildings (Cullingworth 1975). Once again, the general provisions of the Act for control were given effect by Order, produced this time to coincide with the Act's coming into force in April 1933.

As before, a ministerial Circular also spelt out the limits, as central government saw them, of the freedom that local authorities would acquire. However, Circular 1305 (Ministry of Health 1933) does suggest a wider purpose for interim development control than simply allowing development to proceed before a plan was produced. Design and appearance, and scattered development, which are regarded as appropriate matters for planning policy in a scheme, also become by extension subject to interim control. As for the control of uses, although "it will probably be wise ordinarily to limit any control of this kind", the prevention of uses "dangerous to health or detrimental to the neighbourhood or likely to involve the ratepayers in unreasonable expense" are cited as grounds for refusal. Above all, the Circular places emphasis on the need for elasticity for "give and take" in dealings between local authorities and landowners in the interim period, and underlines the discretionary nature of the local authorities' task in control.

The 1932 Act has been criticized for its failure to tackle planning problems adequately and because it removed the requirement, introduced in the 1919 Act, that towns with a population greater than 20000 should produce plans. Such a view overlooks the vastly increased scope of planning policy that the legislation made possible and also, as Cherry (1975) points out, the fact that the obligation to prepare plans had been far from universally respected. Moreover, planning activity in the period 1932–42 greatly exceeded that of the period 1919–32. Activity was greatest in England, with 5 per cent of the country covered by operational schemes by 1942, but far more interesting was the fact that in England 73 per cent of the country's area was subject to a resolution to prepare a plan and thus to interim development control. The proportion was much lower in Scotland and Wales; but, even so, nearly half the country was covered by interim control. The reticence of the early years of the century appears to have given place to a marked enthusiasm for control, if not for plan-making. Yet, from the

19

point of view of development control, the Act had two fundamental weaknesses. The first was that compensation might be payable if planning permission were refused, thereby making it difficult to resist development. The second was the absence of any form of enforcement action except in the context of an approved scheme. A developer did not have to apply for permission under interim control and the local authority could take action only if existing by-laws were flouted or when the scheme was actually in force. Nevertheless, in London at least, Knowles & Pitt (1972) argue that "Architects and the public at large came to understand the necessity for the submission of plans to the [London County] Council" (p. 111). For all that the powers available were permissive, planning control appeared to have caught on.

The pressure for universal control of development

In spite of its weaknesses, the 1932 Act established some very important principles. For the first time, the control of individual decisions on land-use was partially divorced from a system of plans to become, as it were, an activity in its own right. This control was of a very different order from the application of by-laws under the Public Health Act, because it did not necessarily involve the use of dimensional norms and began to concern questions of amenity and activity that were left largely to local authority discretion to determine. It also recognized that the purposes for which a plan was prepared might be undermined by uncontrolled development elsewhere (Cullingworth 1975). Both the success of Act and its limitations were incentives to improve the system and to institute not partial permissive control, but control that was universal and mandatory. The pressure for reform came from several directions and it reflected four separate but interconnected preoccupations.

The first preoccupation was a desire to see strategic controls that reflected national priorities instead of a local, regulatory system of control, and it stems from the reports by Barlow and Uthwatt, published during the Second World War. Montague Barlow had been commissioned by Neville Chamberlain in 1938 to investigate the distribution of population at a national level in the light of the profound changes that were taking place in industry. His report (Barlow 1942) specifically foresaw the need for universal control of decisions to develop, in order to achieve specific objectives for the proper distributions of activities. The need for universal control was given more specific impetus in the Uthwatt report on compensation and betterment (Uthwatt 1942). His criticism of the 1932 Act was that it was local in outlook and "largely regulatory", not giving local authorities the possibility to secure positive development:

Proposals by land owners involving further development of an existing urban area are not likely in practice to be refused by a local authority if the only reason against the development taking place is that from the national standpoint its proper location is elsewhere, particularly when it is remembered that the prevention of any such development might not only involve the authority in having to pay compensation but would, in addition, deprive them of substantial increases in rate income" (para. 14ii).

Uthwatt's view, already expressed in an interim report (Uthwatt 1941), was that a central authority was necessary for the exercise of universal control, which would be strategic and would be able to initiate (not merely respond to) development. The impetus for that view, apart from the experience of the 1932 Act was, according to Cullingworth (1975), the belief that there was widespread speculation on bombed sites that would hamper efforts at reconstruction.

The second preoccupation had to do with the control of land values through the payment of compensation and the collection of betterment, which it was the task of the Uthwatt Committee to resolve. Indeed, this was a problem that had bedevilled the planning system since its inception in 1909. The 1909 Act had recognized that if the state deprived a landowner of a legitimate right to develop, the landowner might reasonably expect to be compensated. Conversely, if the state created higher land values through the activity of creating town extension schemes, it might reasonably expect itself to receive the betterment for the increase in value. Thus, the 1909 Act allowed for the payment of compensation at 100 per cent and the collection of betterment at 50 per cent, the latter a last-minute amendment to the bill in its passage through the House of Lords (Minett 1974). In practice this simple equation was fraught with difficulties. There was, for example, a real difficulty in knowing who might be liable for compensation, which in turn required a definition of when land was "ripe for development". On the other hand, betterment proved difficult to collect and could not in any case equal the claim for compensation. Nevertheless, these arrangements for compensation and betterment were maintained in 1919. The fear of having to pay compensation appears both to have encouraged local authorities to include much more land than was needed in town planning schemes and to permit rather than refuse the development under interim control (Cherry 1975). Although the betterment to be collected was raised to 75 per cent in the 1932 Act (although the Bill had originally allowed for 100 per cent), the basic problems persisted until the war.

Uthwatt's account of the problems associated with compensation and betterment remains unequalled. The debate on the whole question of land values, and the attempts to enforce state control in the interests of national and strategic objectives for development, goes beyond the scope of this book; they have been fully explored elsewhere (Cullingworth 1980, Cox 1984). Nevertheless, Uthwatt's proposals were to have a crucial impact on the development control systems that emerged after the war and can be summarized as follows. The right to compensation should be a once and for all payment to those who could legitimately claim, at the point at which universal control was imposed, that their land had been "dead ripe" for development. All betterment should be returned to the state for the imposition of a betterment tax of 100 per cent. Widespread powers were needed for the compulsory purchase of land for development. In all these activities a central planning authority, not the local authorities, would be the key actor. The explicit intention was to nationalize development rights and to move towards the nationalization of development land.

The third preoccupation during the war years had to do with the proper relationship between a system of plans and a system of development control. The 1932 Act with its extensive possibilities for interim control had, as we have noted, already begun to loosen the relationship. As an immediate response to the problems created by bombing, the 1943 Town and Country (Interim Development) Act gave legislative effect to the desire for universal control, by removing the need for a resolution before control was exercised. By so doing, it called into question the value of having planning schemes at all. On the other hand, under the 1932 Act, where schemes had been produced, there was no further need for an express consent for development. This led to the difficulty that for a development to depart from an operative plan required the plan itself to be modified – a slow and cumbersome procedure. Cullingworth (1975: 84) has shown how official thinking during the war came to see this system of plans as unsatisfactorily static and inflexible. The preferred solution was for universal control to be accompanied by a series of "outline plans" that would give at least some guidance to landowners and developers, if not the degree of certainty that was available under the then current planning schemes.

The fourth preoccupation that lay behind the move to introduce universal control was the question of the appropriate level of decision-making and the concomitant relationship between central and local government. From the beginning, planning control, as an extension of by-law regulatory powers in the nineteenth century, was seen as essentially a creature of the district authorities, with central government keeping more or less control over the approval of planning schemes. Uthwatt and Barlow had both argued in favour of a national planning body in order to be able to keep control over strategy, and Uthwatt accepted that the burden of compensation would be too great for local authorities to bear. Within central government, at least one group of officials was in favour of central control through a land commission. At the same time, to cut local authorities out of the process of control for which they were already responsible seemed unwise. The compromise solution was to favour counties over districts (Cullingworth 1975). This had something to commend it. Regional planning, undertaken at county level, had enjoyed a certain vogue in the inter-war period and, although regional plans were entirely non-statutory, they had been given explicit recognition in Circular 1305. These, and the possibility of joint committees of district authorities, clearly pointed a way forwards that would at least partially circumvent the possibility that parochialism would inhibit appropriate national policy.

The 1947 Town and Country Planning Act

By the end of the war there appeared to be a broad consensus on the need for both universal control and the payment and collection of compensation and betterment. The Coalition government advocated both and produced a White Paper that specifically recommended that the state should be responsible for paying compensation and collecting betterment, even if local authorities would be responsible for dealing with planning applications. The White Paper also advocated compulsory purchase powers to assist in the process of appropriate development (Cullingworth 1975). However, it was the Labour administration of 1945 that gave effect to the proposals in the 1947 Town and Country Planning Act. The Act had five principal aims:

- to make fresh provision for planning the development and use of land
- to make provision for the grant of permission to develop land and for other powers of control over the use of land
- to confer on public authorities additional powers in respect of the acquisition and development of land for planning and other purposes, and to amend the law relating to compensation for the compulsory acquisition of land
- to provide payments out of a central fund for depreciation occasioned by planning restrictions
- to secure the recovery for the benefit of the community of development charges in respect of certain new development.

Although we are used to thinking of the 1947 Act and its successors entirely in terms of the first two aims, in practice the Labour government was far more concerned with the last three. Indeed, it appears to have seen the legislation as leading eventually to the nationalization of land, and the process of development control as again interim, pending not the approval of plans but the community control of land (Cullingworth 1975, Hall 1975). Betterment was set at 100 per cent of the increased value of land, and compensation was payable only for land that was "dead ripe" for development in 1939. A Central Land Board was set up to deal with both on the assumption that payment of compensation would be at least balanced by the collection of betterment.

The principles of universal control

The making of plans and the control of development was, however, left in local authority hands, with the counties and the county boroughs becoming the responsible authorities. They were required to prepare county maps that corresponded roughly to the idea of the outline plan that, as we have seen, was current in official thinking during the war, and where necessary for urban areas, a more detailed town map. Plans, once created, were to be reviewed every five years. For the control of development, the 1947 Act built on the foundations already laid in 1932, although the post-war provisions extended well beyond the scope of pre-war legislation. A key part of the Act that has remained virtually unchanged since was a definition of development. The pre-war inclusion of both building operations and land-use change was maintained, but extended. In defining operations the wording is such as to include not merely buildings but engineering work and mining, as well as waste disposal. For change of use, the word "material" was added, and the Act provided for secondary legislation to define categories of use within which a change could not be a material one. This was to become the Use Classes Order.

The second innovation of the Act was to ensure that all development so defined required planning permission, regardless of the existence of the development plan. This meant that any development that was a departure from a development plan did not require the plan itself to be changed beforehand. The elasticity that had been advocated by government in the 1930s and 1940s was thereby achieved, and the right to develop only conferred by the decision of the responsible authority. This sweeping away of development rights was from the outset somewhat softened by the general granting of permission for certain kinds of minor development by order. The intention was both to remove trivial cases from local authority scrutiny, and to provide a sop for home-owners. The General Development Order, first approved in 1948, thus carries a schedule of what is habitually referred to as permitted development, for which express consent is not required. Important though permitted development rights are, their existence does not obscure the general principle that, since 1947, development rights have been nationalized.

The elasticity that the 1947 Act introduced was further enhanced by a third important innovation. Not only was planning permission required even when there was an approved plan in force, but the criteria by which the planning application would be judged were to be "the provisions of the development plan, so far as material thereto, and . . . any other material considerations" (§14). Finally, the local authority was given the power to impose conditions on planning permission "as they think fit" (§14). Together these form the discretionary basis for the whole of the British development control system, and give the system its unique character. But they also raise a difficult question about the right relationship between forward planning policy and the control of development, and they ensure that there can never be any certainty about potential future development or use of land until planning permission has been granted. Finally, the Act made good the omission of all the previous legislation by installing a system for enforcing planning control.

The Act also resolved the question of the respective roles of central and local government. The Central Land Board was set up to deal with compensation and betterment, and, as envisaged, the counties were left to prepare plans and control development. For development control, however, central government recognized that districts having had a role in development control before the war would, without question, want to continue, and, as a result, arrangements were made for delegation of powers to joint boards, which might operate within part of a county area. For the rest, central government took various kinds of long-stop role. It retained rights to interfere in both policy-making and control. It was to be responsible for approving plans. All applications for departures from development plans in force would have been referred to central government. And it retained a very widely drawn right itself to deal with applications.

Circular 1305 had already established the Circular as a key element in planning policy and this was to be reinforced by the practice of development control after 1947. Central government declined to become entangled in the specifics of particular cases, using its powers sparingly; but it took an increasing interest in spelling out how it saw local authorities discharging their duties in general terms. The role of arbiter was again a continuation of pre-war practice. But after 1947 with all development requiring a valid planning permission, the scope for dispute was vastly increased, and a right of appeal to the minister against local authorities' decisions became the *quid pro quo* for the nationalization of development rights. This in turn gave central government an important power to adjudicate on what might be construed as material considerations in development control.

The 1947 Act was thus born of the experience of the 1932 legislation, but broke definitively with the last vestiges of a zoning system in favour of discretionary action by local authorities under the watchful eye of central government. By requiring a permission for all development and placing an obligation on local authorities to reflect on the material considerations of an application, whether contained in a plan or not, the Act had nationalized development rights. The development plan did not identify rights to develop; it merely indicated the likelihood of permission being granted. In the name of elasticity and flexibility, the legislation had reduced the certainty for developers and landowners. But by implication it offered the possibility of negotiating the material considerations.

The maturing of the control system

The 1950s and 1960s were to prove to be the quiet years of the development control system. It was a period during which the system matured and administrative practices were developed. It was also a period in which the limits of the Town and Country Planning Act were tested by the courts. Thus, demolition was held to be usually outside the definition of development, a decision that confirmed a policy stance in a Circular in 1949 (McAuslan 1975). It was a period in which the scope of material considerations was explored, and limits set on the freedom to impose conditions (Bowhill 1980). Finally, development control acquired the reputation as a mind-numbing bureaucratic activity, somewhat less worthy than the process of plan preparation:

> Development control goes on everywhere all the time, for the most part in happy disregard of the deep and important matters discussed in the last chapter [Development Plans] . . . There is something very Parkinsonian about development control. It inexorably fills the time available for its performance. Much of this time is not spent on professional inspection, measure-

ment, thought and writing, but on consultations and formalities. (Keeble 1983: 105)

The focus of attention was by and large elsewhere. First and foremost, the system for paying compensation and collecting betterment proved enormously contentious and its implementation led to serious problems. Although there had been general acceptance for the need for a universal planning system, the Conservatives, returned to power in 1951, were opposed to the collection of betterment, and this part of the 1947 Act was repealed in 1954. Curiously, however, the ability of local authorities to purchase land at existing-use value persisted until 1959. On the other hand, there was no attempt to introduce a continuing right to compensation. Thus, while the nationalization of development land became an evermore distant objective, the nationalization of development rights remained intact. This inevitably began to raise the profile of the development control provisions of the Act.

Furthermore, the growing preoccupation was with the system of plans. Two separate issues were involved. First was the question of speed. Far from a complete set of plans being in place by 1950, with reviews taking place every five years thereafter, complete coverage was never achieved before the system was changed in 1968. The second issue was to do with the nature of the plans themselves. Although official intentions had been towards "outline plans" in the war years, both county and town maps were based on the Ordnance Survey, and the precise limits came to seem unresponsive to local needs. At one level, the county maps were insufficiently strategic and too fixed in describing a status quo; at the other, town maps failed to offer enough detail to reflect the complexities of urban areas or the realities of the development process.

The limitations of the 1947 development plan system led eventually to reforms. In 1963 the Planning Advisory Group was set up to investigate the system of plans, and out of their review emerged the system of structure and local plans that has endured more or less to the present day. However, the Group did reflect briefly on development control, arguing that the experience since the War had been largely positive and demonstrated the system's strength:

> In our view, however, the main defect of the present planning system lies not in the methods of control, but in the development plans on which they are based and they are intended to implement. (Planning Advisory Group 1965: para. 1.15)

Nevertheless, they did note that the system was "too complicated" and "too slow" and that there were wide variations in performance. Management appeared to be the key issue, not the system itself. This in turn led to the commissioning of a management study that reported in 1967 (Ministry of Housing and Local Government 1967). This apparently uncontentious review made a series of recommendations that were implemented by legislative change and policy advice. Perhaps its greatest significance, however, was the way in which it set the agenda for reviewing development control in the 15 years that followed its publication, by placing the emphasis firmly upon performance, not upon the objectives of controlling development. It perhaps helped to engrain the notion that development control was cumbersome and bureaucratic, and in that way a brake upon legitimate development.

The system under scrutiny: Dobry and the Expenditure Committee

The attitude to development control that the Planning Advisory Group and management study reports represented was to return with a vengeance in the much more difficult circumstances of the early 1970s. This time a noted barrister, George Dobry, was commissioned in 1973 to investigate the problem. Dobry was given a wide-ranging brief "to consider whether the development control system . . . adequately meets current needs and to advise on the lines on which it might be improved . . ." (Dobry 1975). He was also asked to review procedures for appeal. In spite of this open-ended brief, the resulting report took, as Harrison (1975) has noted, an essentially orthodox approach that in the main considered the procedures and not the objects of the control system. Although concluding the system was "potentially very good", Dobry argued that the procedures did not adequately meet current needs: "Regrettably, the system is slow, even at times desperately slow, because its procedures are, as at present used, too cumbersome" (para. 1.9). He therefore recommended a series of procedural changes, of which the most significant was a streamlined system for minor applications, with a possibility of a deemed approval after a six-week period. The one recommendation that did go further than procedure was that demolition should be brought within the scope of control, to prevent premature demolition, ugly gap sites and the possibility of developers exercising leverage over local authority decision-making (Dobry 1974).

The circumstances of the Dobry report go a long way to explaining the heavy emphasis placed upon the problem of delay. As he himself noted, the number of applications received annually in England and Wales had averaged some 400000 throughout the 1960s. In the early 1970s the repeal of controls on office development and expansion of money supply, led to an unprecedented boom in land and property prices. This in turn led to an unprecedented rise in planning applications, which reached 623000 by 1972, an increase of more than 50 per cent over the average figure for the 1960s, achieved in a mere two years. There was no question but that a system geared to cope with one level of applications would come under severe strain with such a rapid increase. The debate over delay was thus given an added edge, which was further sharpened by the fact that the political consensus on the need for development control was falling apart. More and more the delay that local authorities' discretion seemed to create was seen as a product of a municipal socialism to which the economic liberalism of the early years of the Heath administration was opposed.

The Department of the Environment's (DOE's) unwillingness to make major changes as a result of the Dobry Report only served to fuel the controversy. The DoE did not, for example, accept either of the two major recommendations. In their view, dividing applications into major and minor would have created more problems than it would have solved, and control of demolition would have introduced an unwelcome extra administrative burden when the emphasis needed to be upon reducing delay (DoE 1975). The result was that the increasing pressure to do something about what was seen as the nefarious consequences of development control was in no way satisfied. Less than 12 months after the government's response to the Dobry Report, the House of Commons' Expenditure Committee began its own inquiry into planning procedures with, as they put it, "a view to identifying reasons for delays and the resource costs that such delays create" (House of Commons 1977: para. 2). The Committee's most notable conclusions were the need to appoint Planning Assessors to help local authorities monitor their performance, and the need to review the system of development plans, because of the length of time that preparing structure and local plans had taken.

However, the Report is far more notable for the wealth of evidence that the Committee received than for its conclusions. Two issues stand out, both in the written submissions and the accounts of the oral evidence given. The first was the overwhelming concern for delay in the system. The second was for what was frequently regarded as the unjustifiable detailed interference by local authorities in matters of design. The two came together in the evidence on development at Queens Park, Billericay, in which a developer was caught between the conflicting design requirements of the district and Essex County Council (House of Commons 1977, vol. II: 387–401). As a whole, the Expenditure Committee's work brought together bodies such as the Royal Institution of Chartered Surveyors and Royal Institute of British Architects, with the House Builders' Federation and developers' representatives, all of whom pointed to the cost of delay and to the need to reduce local authority interference in legitimate development. Local planning authorities were seen to be using their wide discretionary power arbitrarily. The only really spirited defence of development control was offered not by the Royal Town Planning Institute but by the Civic Trust.

The Expenditure Committee's approach was further underscored by two reports from the private sector in the late 1970s. Moor & Langton (1978) detailed nine cases of development in which delay appeared to have been excessive. In the following year the developers Slough Estates (1979) attempted to compare the process of obtaining planning permission for factory building in Britain with the process elsewhere. The study concluded that what could take 26 weeks to gain approval here could be achieved in a mere four-and-a-half weeks in the USA. Yet none of this produced much action from the Labour government, which was preoccupied with the problems of the economy. The one action it did take, to increase the scope of permitted development rights by amending the General Development Order, resulted in an embarrassing débâcle in the House of Lords (*Journal of Planning and Environment Law* 1978), and the Amendment Order had to be withdrawn.

Development control and local government reform

The detailed examination of development control by Dobry and the Expenditure Committee must also be set against the background of a major change in local government structure and responsibilities. In devising their proposals for a new system of development plans, the Planning Advisory Group were working on the assumption that reform, then already under consideration, would lead to the abolition of counties and districts and their replacement by unitary authorities. One level of local government would prepare structure and local plans, and be responsible for development control. In fact after much debate, and after three separate reports, the Local Government Act 1972 perpetuated a two-tier structure, with counties retaining their ancient boundaries in much of the country, and districts, considerably larger than their predecessors, at the lower level. In the major conurbations, new Metropolitan Counties were established, with districts analogous to the London boroughs that had been created ten years before (Hampton 1987).

Planning powers were divided between the tiers. Counties became the strategic planning authority and they prepared structure plans. However, districts took over the preparation of local plans, and acquired most of the control function. The relationship between the tiers in the first ten years after the change were not always easy. Counties, jealous of the planning strategies they were required to prepare, suspected districts of irresponsibility in taking development control decisions. Districts objected to meddling in what they believed to be their preserve. Until 1980, counties had the right to direct a refusal where they believed a proposed development would adversely affect strategic policy, and in some cases insisted on seeing every planning application to ensure that districts did not act waywardly. This soured relationships and without question added to the time it took to process planning applications. The power of counties to direct decisions was repealed in 1980, and there was some fear at the time that strategic policy might be more than ever difficult to maintain. But in practice, local authorities were in the main beginning to work more harmoniously. A code of practice was produced. And in any case the major concern of local planning authorities had by the 1980s shifted elsewhere.

Reform under the Conservative government

The agenda that had been set for the debate on development control during the 1960s drew enthusiastic support from the Conservative government under Margaret Thatcher, which was returned to power in 1979. Deeply committed to turning back what they saw as the creeping socialism of the Labour government, and to avoiding the economic about-turn under the Conservative government of Edward Heath, the Conservatives promoted the ideal of the market as the best regulator of human activity. This in turn led to a view that government at both

29

central and local levels had been too much involved in the day-to-day running of the country, with the result that individual freedom to choose had been eroded. In Conservative philosophy the objective of government should be to create the conditions under which the market could flourish. In the memorable, if ambiguous, phrase of William Hague, now Secretary of State for Wales, but at the time a 16 year old delegate to the 1977 Conservative Party Conference, the duty of government should be to "roll back the frontiers of the state". It was ironic that this desire to return the power to choose to the grass roots and to create the conditions under which the free market could flourish turned out to mean increasing control from the centre.

Local government in general, and planning activity in particular, fell foul of this free-market nostrum. But it did not mean that the Conservative government had a coherent view of the planning system or of the control of development. Changes were introduced piecemeal and were partial in effect, and the most significant were to be in terms of policy rather than new legislation.

Legislative and policy change

One such change had to do with the consequential effect of changes to local government. These included the setting up of the Urban Development Corporations to deal with the regeneration of inner-city areas in all the country's major cities. Among other things, these corporations took on the local planning authority's development control powers. The abolition of the Greater London Council and the six metropolitan councils in 1984 had less direct bearing on development control, but did remove the capacity to prepare structure plans. These were then replaced by the obligation on metropolitan districts and the London boroughs to produce unitary development plans that would contain both strategic and local land-use policy.

The other had to do with the direct legislative changes that were made to the planning system. First of all, the Conservative government achieved what their predecessors had failed to, in amending the General Development Order to allow more freedom to householders in particular. The aim was to reduce the number of applications received by local planning authorities, but the effect was also to make permitted development rights more difficult to apply, because of the exceptions to the new limits that were made for Conservation Areas, Areas of Outstanding Natural Beauty, and National Parks. More significant was the introduction of, first, Enterprise Zones, and then Simplified Planning Zones, in which development was permitted as of right, provided it conformed to the general conditions of the document that covered the zone. Enterprise Zones were introduced to allow industry to develop free from normal restrictions, but the most significant freedom was from local taxation for a period of ten years. Simplified Planning Zones only offered freedom from the normal process of development control by permitting development, provided it conformed to the general requirements on use of land that was spelt out in zone document. These were in effect a return to the zoning system that had operated before 1947, but in general their direct impact on planning and development control has been limited, except in specific areas.

The final legislative change had to do with the amendment to the Use Classes Order of 1988. The Order, which since its inception in 1948 had been the mechanism for resolving difficulties about what was and what was not a material change, was in need of reform. The DOE Property Advisory Group was asked to report (Property Advisory Group 1985); its proposals were substantially modified in the eventual order (*Planning* 1986). However, its major innovation was one that stemmed from the original report. A new Business Class (B1) would allow the use of a building for offices, for research and development, or for industrial purposes that did not carry the risk of pollution, without the need for planning permission. This change, which appeared to go well beyond the original intention of the Order, was justified both by the need to encourage economic development and by the changing nature of high-technology industry.

The sum total of legislative change must be regarded as marginal rather than wholesale: the 1980s ended with the development control system substantially intact. All of these legislative changes signalled a policy attitude that alarmed local authorities, however. It encouraged local authorities, if it did not actually require them, to take a stance strongly in favour of development. It cast the local planning authorities in the role of enablers, not controllers. It down-played the importance of locally prepared policy in development plans.

The policy attitude implicit in the reasoning behind legislation was spelt out in more detail in the Circulars issued by the DOE in the early 1980s. This policy advice was considerably more insidious than changes to the statutes, because it created a framework that was all embracing but ill defined, but which was nevertheless a material consideration in determining planning applications. The general policy tone has been set by a series of White Papers, whose very titles indicated their intention: *Releasing enterprise, Building businesses . . . not barriers*, and *Lifting the burden* (Cabinet Office 1985, DOE 1985, DTI 1988), all of which suggests that the government's task has to be to minimize constraints on innovative enterprise. This in turn came to influence attitudes to the planning system, and in particular the proposal to reform the development plan system contained in the consultation paper, *The future of development plans*. Thatcher's first Secretary of State for the Environment, Michael Heseltine, had already given a clear indication of the government's attitude to the planning authorities in 1980, in Circular 22/80 (DOE 1980), which was loathed by the planning profession for its stridency, although the final version was somewhat more muted than the draft (Thornley 1991). In general it criticized the poor performance of local authorities, and in particular exhorted local authorities to be less concerned with detail in the control of design. The actual import of this advice was ambiguous, but it was used by the developers to justify appeals against local authorities who had used design grounds to refuse an application.

Perhaps more significant were the Circulars on industrial development and housing land. Circular 22/80 had already required that local authorities identify a five-year rolling supply of land for housing – itself a requirement that had originated under the Labour administration in the late 1970s. But the Circular went on to assert:

> The fact that the house building needs of the area can be met from identified sites is not in itself sufficient reason for refusing planning permission elsewhere. (DoE 1980: Annex A, para. 7).

That message was reinforced in Circular 15/84:

> Planning applications for housing should be considered on their merits, having regard to the provisions of the development plan *and* other material considerations. The result of land availability studies should continue to be treated as a material consideration in determining planning appeals. It is not the intention, however, that decisions on individual planning applications should turn on a precise calculation of whether the supply of identified sites for housing exactly matches or varies from the five-year provision derived from the structure or local plan. Such calculations can rarely be exact, bearing in mind the constraints on land becoming available, the incidence of infill and other small sites, and variations in the capacity of allocated sites. (DoE 1984a: para. 18)

In the same year, the Circular on industrial development gave much the same emphasis on the discretion available to local authorities:

> . . . where a developer applies for permission for a development which is contrary to the proposals for an approved development plan, this does not, in itself, justify a refusal of permission . . . (DoE 1984b: para. 9)

This advice was particularly threatening to the relationship between development control decisions and policy contained in plans, quite apart from its effect on the morale of the planning profession. By dwelling on the discretion that was available to local authorities, it tugged at the very point at which the British system was already weak. This was particularly vexatious for local authorities in the case of housing land. Because of the pressure from housebuilders, under the Labour government in the late 1970s, local authorities had already been required to identify a rolling supply of housing land in agreement with developers and landowners, quite apart from the normal process of land allocation in development plans. What value could such a process have now, they asked, if they were also to grant permission for land not part of the rolling programme?

The change of heart: the Planning and Compensation Act

The end of the 1980s witnessed what appeared to be an about-turn by the government, culminating in the Planning and Compensation Act 1991, which reconfirmed the status of development plans and introduced what has been dubbed the "plan-led" approach to planning. At heart the unavoidable problem was that a theological approach to policy offered no coherent view of how the planning system could work. Three factors seemed to have swayed the government in changing its mind about planning.

The first was a series of public inquiries in the mid-1980s that proved particularly embarrassing for the government. Encouraged by the tenor of central government advice in Circular 15/84, a group of developers came together as Consortium Developments to propose several major new housing developments in the southeast, which would be designed to offer a full range of services in addition to the housing, thus tapping a renewed interest in the idea of the balanced community. The first of these, at Tillingham Hall in Essex, was in the metropolitan green belt, mid-way between Upminister and Basildon. The developers' argument was that there was a demonstrable need for housing, that the proposed settlement was fully self-contained and that the green belt land was not particularly attractive. The second, at Foxley Wood in Hampshire, was not in a green belt, but in land that was not identified for future development. The local authorities' argument was that enough land was available elsewhere in the county, and that the location in northeast Hampshire was not identified as an area of growth in the structure plan. Both developments aroused widespread local opposition from residents and elected representatives, who were in the main Conservative. Both developments were eventually refused, although, in the case of Foxley Wood, only after much ministerial soul-searching.

The second factor was the attitude of the development industry itself. Even in the early 1980s, housebuilders were arguing that planning had a role to play for them in identifying land for future development. Tom Baron, then Chairman of Whelmar, a major national housebuilder, who was appointed as special advisor to Michael Heseltine, although thoroughly critical of the way in which planning operated, nevertheless did not advocate its disappearance (Baron 1980). A decade later, the House Builders' Federation was taking a notably more conciliatory line, and arguing for the retention of structure plans that central government had originally intended to abandon (Humber 1989, Parliament 1989). As Haar (1989) has put it in relation to the USA, developers by and large support planning for the way in which it regulates an otherwise chaotic market in land.

The third factor is to be inferred rather than directly identified from policy statements, and has to do with the difficulty of discretionary power. The problem for central government, in advocating that local authorities take maximum advantage of the discretion available under the Planning Acts, was that it also opened the way for wilful action by local authorities that might arouse opposition. Plans came to be seen as a way in which disputes are more easily resolved and the means by which local authorities could be held to account for future action.

The result was the introduction into the Planning and Compensation Bill of a clause that made the development plan the first consideration in determining planning applications. This clause was given more weight by the fact that the Bill also required the production of district-wide local plans to ensure that the whole country was covered by detailed planning documents. Nevertheless, the introduction of what was to become Section 54A of the Town and Country Planning Act was a curious one. It started life as an Opposition amendment that was picked up eagerly by Sir George Young, the Minister responsible for shepherding the Bill through parliament, and its final wording was stronger than the Labour amendment itself:

> Where, in making a determination under the Planning Acts, regard is to be had to the development plan, the determination shall be in accordance with the plan unless material considerations indicate otherwise.

Quite how this Section is to be interpreted is far from clear. Ostensibly it brings development control decisions much closer to the committed policy in the plan. Yet this is in no sense a return to a zoning system, because the reference to other material considerations remains. In reaching decisions, local authorities would still have to weigh plan policy against the circumstances of place and time and the particular characteristics of the proposed development. Nevertheless, the interpretation that has gained ground is that it represents an important shift of policy. Whereas, after 1947, successive governments insisted upon a policy presumption in favour of development, ministers in 1991 talked about a policy presumption in favour of development in accordance with the plan (Grant 1991). Quite what this will mean in practice for development control decisions is still not yet clear. But it has been interpreted as making it essential for developers and landowners to ensure that policy in plans reflects their interests. This has dramatically increased the rate of objection to plans out for consultation, and the deposit version of the unitary development plan for Leeds has led to more than 2000 objections being lodged (*Planning Week* 1994). This is no doubt set to become the pattern.

This latest development in the evolution of the British development control system raises once again the relationship between policy, plans and decisions to be taken on individual cases. It begs the question of how much detail can be committed in advance in a plan and how much elasticity or flexibility is needed to cope with the unforeseen. It raises the issue of how policy is to be expressed in plans, and what criteria might be used to evaluate the implementation of that policy. It also raises the issue of the limits of discretion and how that discretion should be accounted for. These difficult issues form the basis of later chapters.

British development control in a wider context: the development industry, central–local relations and administrative law

Before we turn to compare Britain with France and other countries, three general points about the British system need to be made. The first of these has to do with the relationship between systems of control and the development industry. The second concerns the relationship of the development control systems to an emerging pattern of local administration, and the relationship between local and central government. The third is about the relationship between planning legislation, emerging views on administrative law and discretionary power. All three are important in the way that they have shaped development control.

Development control and the development industry

What is striking about the evolution of the British system of land-use control is the way in which it has responded to a powerful and increasingly well organized private sector. Charles I intervened extensively in the development of Covent Garden, but he did not take direct control of the development, and that pattern of regulation, rather than direct intervention, was confirmed by the London Rebuilding Act. The history of development in London was in many ways a happy conjunction of regulatory control with landowners and builders, who found it very much in their interest to play along with the controls imposed. The controls could not have succeeded without that acquiescence, and where it was lacking, away from the great estates, the quality of the development produced was often doubtful. The pattern persisted into the nineteenth century. Even housing put up for the working classes was not often intrinsically poor: the problems had more to do with overcrowding and poor repair of older property than with the quality of building and layout. When, by the end of the nineteenth century, public opinion acknowledged that greater control needed to be exercised, not only over the form and layout of housing but also over strategic questions of locations and densities, a well organized industry was able to respond efficiently and promptly, first to by-law regulations and then to density control and planning schemes, because it was in their interest to do so. The form of housing in the private sector changed radically in response to the preferred forms of housing in the Ministry of Health Handbook, which was primarily aimed at the public sector (Ministry of Health 1919).

But the desire to take control of strategic decisions on the use of land, which required control of all development and led to the nationalization of development rights after 1947, leads to a new shift in this relationship. First, it divided the right to current use from the right to the further development of land, a division that does not exist as a matter of principle in the same way in other countries. Secondly, it led to attempts to protect rights of landownership and limit the growth of local authority discretion. Because of the lack of constitutional rights

35

to landownership, the planning system has been developed to provide redress specifically for landowners and developers, but not for members of the public. Third-party rights to challenge local authority decisions are very limited, but an applicant refused planning permission always has the right of appeal. Moreover, the challenges to the planning system through the courts have all tended to define the parameters of local authority discretion (McAuslan 1980). As an example, the apparently unbounded power given to local authorities to impose conditions "as they think fit" (Town and Country Planning Act 1990: §70) has been the subject of successive judgements that substantially limit that power (Bowhill 1980).

Another aspect of the relationship between public control and the private sector of landowner and developers has been the growth of a negotiative approach to development control decisions. The possibility for a local authority to determine the material considerations that apply does by implication give the developers scope for arguing their own case. In addition, the 1947 Act introduced a general power for local authorities to enter into agreements with the developers "for the purpose of restricting or regulating the development or use of land" (Town and Country Planning Act 1947: §25). At first this was a power relatively little used, because it required approval by the minister. The 1967 Management Study (MoHLG 1967) recommended that this need for ministerial approval be removed, and the law was changed in 1968. Since then, agreements have both found a useful place in local authorities' armoury and provided a high point of alarm and muddled thinking on the part of those who saw this as local authority discretion taken too far (Loughlin 1990). An attempt to try to define the scope of agreements as a result of a report by the DoE Property Advisory Group (Property Advisory Group 1983, DoE 1983) was criticized at the time (Grant 1984). More recent research has shown that, by and large, local authorities have acted prudently in using agreements and that agreements have been used to secure necessary improvements to infrastructure rather than to sell planning permissions for unrelated fringe benefits, a major fear of critics of such agreements (DoE 1992).

Yet this story has taken a further twist with the passing of the Planning and Compensation Act. This introduced the possibility of developers undertaking unilateral obligations to restrict development or to carry out work on land or to make payments to the local authority. As a matter of policy the Minister declared that the willingness to enter such an obligation would be a material consideration at appeal. There is a certain irony in the way in which the government appears to have moved from criticizing local authorities for trying to sell planning permission to one that could be seen as encouraging developers to buy it. These fears have surfaced in the case of superstore applications at Plymouth, where the decision seems to have rested on the extent of benefits that the preferred developers were prepared to offer (*Journal of Planning and Environment Law* 1994).

Local discretion and central control

Until the nineteenth century, the mechanisms for implementing control were ad hoc or non-existent. Historically the units of local authority that have existed from the Middle Ages may have had few powers, but were subject to very little central control of their activities (Richards 1981). The reform and modernization of local government in the nineteenth century was very largely a response to the social and urbanization problems of the Industrial Revolution (Hampton 1987) and there was pressure from local authorities for increased powers to deal with sanitation and housing, which led in turn to the legislation already referred to. By the end of the nineteenth century there was general recognition that local government, whether at county or district level, was a proper locus for such decision-making. Thus, the 1888 and 1894 Acts that set up the system that endured until 1972 produced a form of local government empowered to deal in Lagroye & Wright's (1979) words with a "residual domain" of activity that central government was unable or unwilling to deal with. There was no general freedom given to local authorities to act, only a series of powers conferred by Parliament in successive legislation.

Yet as Hampton (1987: 18) remarks "This dream of decentralisation as a means of efficiency . . . always wakes to the realities of political control". In the field of development control we have seen in particular how central government has sought to influence how control is exercised by policy directives contained in Circulars or advice notes. These have had an increasingly important bearing on the way in which local authorities discharge their responsibilities. To some extent local authorities welcome the advice that Circulars may contain, but their impact in imposing a political view from the centre during the 1980s has been noted. Court rulings have upheld the need to take full account of Circulars in taking appeal decisions (Thornley 1991) and Davies and his colleagues (1986) were alarmed by the possibility that generalized but all-embracing policy in Circulars might override local – and democratically approved – policy in plans. Enthusiasm for the plan-led system of the Planning and Compensation Act arose possibly because it appeared to increase both power to make and to implement policy. At the same time, however, central government has taken an increasing interest in setting the framework within which plans are prepared, through regional guidance, and by vetting the plans produced by individual local authorities.

A final aspect of local–central relationships that has specific relevance to the development control system is the use of tribunals or public inquiries. As Wraith & Lamb (1971) have shown, from their inception in the nineteenth century, the use of tribunals has had a twofold objective. One was to inform central government by inquiring into circumstances on the spot. The other was to adjudicate in the case of dispute. Both functions were combined in dealing with the parliamentary procedure for enclosures. Their relevance to planning, which essentially concerned local issues, was already apparent to the originators of the 1909 Act. Since 1947 the inquiry has been used as a way both of adjudicating between local

37

authorities and applicants in cases of appeal and informing the Secretary of State in those cases in which the decision is called in. By implication it has had a key role in requiring local authorities to account for and justify their decision-making. Although originally a direct function of central administration, the procedure for inquiries has increasingly become independent of both central and local government. For all that the Inspectorate was until 1992 a part of the Departments of the Environment and Transport, it took care to distance itself from its masters: its headquarters have been in Bristol since 1977. Moreover, the professionalism of the inspectors and the transparency of the proceedings have ensured continued respect for the mechanism.

All this falls into a much wider debate about administrative tribunals and their uses, which goes well beyond the question of town planning and was given prominence by the Franks Commission (Harlow & Rawlings 1984).

Planning legislation, administrative law and discretionary power

The traditional view in this country, expressed by the nineteenth century theorist Dicey was that there was no such thing as administrative law in England and that the state had no special legal status "which was subject to the ordinary law as applied to the ordinary courts" (Loughlin 1985: 123). The rule of law was paramount and Dicey sought to protect the authority of law from the challenge of social legislation. This Loughlin describes as the normativist theory of law, which he contrasts with the functionalist approach that "attempts to break down the dichotomy between administration/discretion/policy and law/rules/rights":

> The key themes in this [functionalist] analysis . . . are first the restrictiveness of the *ultra vires* doctrine; second, the inadequacies or limitations of the courts as supervisory bodies; third, the potential superiority of administrative methods of review; fourth, a need to entrust local authorities with sufficient powers to enable them effectively to provide public services that meet the needs of their constituencies; and finally, the need for an efficient system of supervision by central government in order to resolve conflicts between divergent or contradictory local policies. (Loughlin 1985: 125–6)

The development of planning legislation in the twentieth century falls clearly into the functionalist mode: the wide discretion of the 1947 Act conferred on local authorities had been the fruit of experience of the period 1919–39. Yet at the same time the courts, although excluded from most dispute resolutions because of the possibility of administrative appeal, have been at pains to define the limits of that discretion. Thus, in the best traditions of the British legal system, case law has built up, which defines the scope of action local authorities are empowered to take.

But we are clearly getting into deep water here. As Harlow & Rawlings put it in their opening words: "Behind every theory of administrative law there lies a theory of the state" (1984: 1). We cannot divorce the discussion of planning law from general constitutional theory, or from a consideration of the respective duties and powers of central and local government. In particular, the issue of discretion exercised by public bodies becomes of key significance in the discussion on law. These themes are explored below. What may be said at this stage, however, is that the slowly emerging pattern of British development control is both moulded by, and to some extent is itself moulding, the pattern of government.

CHAPTER 3
France

If, in describing the way in which the British development control system has evolved, the key words that occur again and again are elasticity, flexibility and discretion, with the French system, it is certainty, legality and precision that have informed the process. This in itself suggests a fundamental difference of approach to the control of development, which has affected both the nature of the system and to some extent the objects of control. The most intriguing part of the comparison is the way that two systems built upon entirely different premises nevertheless cope with an essentially similar set of problems, an issue that forms the basis of much of the rest of this book. The reasons for these fundamental differences of approach can be found at many levels. In part it is a question of underlying philosophies that inform much of the culture of the two countries: the French preference for abstract theoretical principles, and British pragmatism. However, much can be ascribed to the political and administrative culture of the two countries, and the thrust of this book is to present an explanation that relates theories and practice of development control to the wider arena of decision-making and government. Nevertheless, in spite of the enormous differences of attitude, perception and practice that exist in the 1990s, the starting point for the two systems is, at least superficially, remarkably similar: the creation of a piazza and the formalization of controls over building.

The origins of the French development control system

The Edict of Nantes had brought peace to a country that for the latter part of the sixteenth century had been torn by the wars of religion. Henri IV, as author of that peace, was able to establish his ascendancy over the whole kingdom, in part through a programme of public works and, in particular, in the embellishment of Paris. As a contemporary observed, "He wanted to make a world of the town, and a miracle of that world, in which he surely imparts to us a love greater than that of a father." (Babelon 1982: 830). The most spectacular of those interventions was the first: the Place Royale, today the Place des Vosges.

Royal intervention and regulatory control

The royal domain of Tournelles to the east of medieval Paris had been abandoned by the widow of Henri II, Catherine de Médicis, after the death of her husband. She had tried to establish a subdivision that had failed because of its distance from the centre; the site became a wasteland given over to the sale of horses. It was on the Parc de Tournelles that Henri IV carried out his experiment in city planning from 1605 onwards and Sully was charged with carrying out the project, which consisted of lots to be sold off around a central square. Purchasers of the lots were required to conform to detailed architectural control and were limited in the use they could make of the buildings once completed. The result was a uniform architectural composition with a continuously arcaded ground floor and upper floors in brick decorated with stone pilasters. The model for the Place Royale were similar squares in Metz, Nancy and Pont-à-Mousson (Chartier & Neveux 1981); Henri IV had seen and admired the square at Metz two years before during a tour of Lorraine (Babelon 1982). Place Royale was finished in 1612, during which time the second of Henri IV's experiments, the triangular Place Dauphine on the Île de la Cité, had been built in the same manner. The resemblance of both to the architecture of the houses in Covent Garden is in all probability not coincidental.

The other effort of Henri IV to improve the quality of his capital was in the introduction of regulations affecting building lines. Since the Middle Ages, regulations had existed in Paris, and a system for their implementation was in place. Streets were required to be at least 7 m in width and buildings no more than 12 m in height. In charge of ensuring conformity to these regulations was the post of *voyer*, whose responsibilities were essentially over roads rather than buildings (Trintignac 1964). These regulations appeared to be frequently ignored by landowners and the imposition of new building lines was thus rarely achieved (Chartier & Neveux 1982). Henri IV saw the reconstitution of these regulations as part of his duty to the capital. But it was left to Sully in his capacity as *grand voyer* to produce for the edict of 1607 a set of regulations and a system of enforcing them. The principle once again was to establish building lines and for building height to be imposed on rebuilding, and instituted what was in effect the first formal system of *permis de construire* (permissions to build) (Bastié 1964). The regulations forbade the overhangs and jettyings of medieval architecture (Babelon 1982) and outlawed the use of wood in favour of stone for structural piers and lintels, and brick or plastered block infill. Such limits on materials were not new but once again had been widely flouted in the sixteenth century (Chartier & Neveux 1982). By contrast, in the seventeenth century the application of the edict of 1607 led to a rapid transformation of powers from a city built of timber to one in which stone and brick predominated.

A final attempt at regulation (not specifically an introduction of Henri IV) was the edict limiting the growth of Paris and the other large towns. Bastié notes that there were 11 such texts issued between 1548 and the Revolution, which prohibited building outside given limits; as with the equivalent decrees of Elizabeth I and the Stuart monarchs, they were largely ineffective. Nevertheless, there was a tendency for urban densities to increase during the seventeenth and eighteenth centuries, largely through the addition of extra floors, but it appears that this was unlikely to have been attributable to controls on building.

The intervention of Henri IV in the Places Royale and Dauphine and the use of regulatory control for rebuilding, as well as the limiting of peripheral development, all find echoes in the comparable activity in London. Yet there are distinct differences that already begin to mark the divergences between English and French practice. Although the form of development at Covent Garden and Place Royale and the intentions behind the developments were broadly similar, the form of intervention was not. Henri IV himself promoted the layout of Place Royale on land already in his ownership and thus characterized the interventionist approach of the French state in the control of promotion and development. At Covent Garden the initiative was essentially that of the Earl of Bedford, even if Charles I leant hard upon the Earl to adopt a particular architectural idiom. Moreover, Covent Garden remained an isolated event; the other achievements of the Commission on Buildings were small by comparison.

The regulatory approach of the 1607 edict was also rather different from that of the London Building Acts. In many ways, France, or at least Paris, appears to have been a century in advance in setting up detailed regulations for new buildings and a system for enforcing them. England lacked a formalized system of building permits until the nineteenth century and, except in the period immediately following the Great Fire, adequate means of inspection were not put in place until the end of the eighteenth century. Yet despite centralized bureaucratic control, which was essentially far more modern than its English counterpart, the transformation of medieval Paris was until the nineteenth century far less dramatic than changes that overtook medieval London. One factor was the nature of the regulations themselves. Although fire was an inherent risk and a frequent occurrence in late medieval Paris, Paris did not suffer from a disaster as severe as London's Great Fire, and whereas in 1666 London was still essentially a "city of sticks", Paris had already been substantially rebuilt piecemeal in brick and stone. French regulations thus aimed at creating new *alignments* (building lines) and forbidding timber construction, but unlike the Rebuilding Act, did not specify constructional standards.

A second significant factor was the pattern of land development. In London, the commodification of the housing market led to a convergence of short-term interests of builders and the long-term interests of landowners in producing high-quality layouts that reflected the fashion for piazzas and classical detailing. In Paris, land tenure appears to have remained distinctly feudal, with the city divided between seigneurial holdings, of which the most important were the Crown, the Archbishopric and the abbey of St-Germain des Prés. The effect of this form of tenure was felt in the levy of *lods et ventes*, which were premiums expressed as a percentage fixed by custom on all sales of property by the seigneurial proprietor.

There appears to have been no equivalent interest in the capital value of the land-holding or by and large in the promotion of development, and the *lods et ventes* apparently had a depressive effect on the land market (Chartier & Neveux 1981).

Elsewhere, other feudal patterns subsisted. In Caen, land might still be offered in the eighteenth century on perpetual leases, a form of tenure that in London was already considered archaic at the start of the seventeenth century (Le Roy Ladurie 1981). Development and redevelopment thus took place by and large on small plots that remained highly resistant to change and there was no apparent incentive to create a building industry dealing in increasingly large units, as in London. In London the crisis of the Great Fire led to the rapid, if pragmatic, amelioration of the built fabric in the City, with building lines and heights controlled by the surveyors, and spacious developments on the estates in the suburban West End, promoted by landowners and developers whose interests coincided. In Paris, development proved far more difficult to control in spite of a superior administrative structure, because there was no incentive to comply. In particular, land that was required for the respect of building line control was simply subsumed into the highway without compensation (Bergel 1973).

The pattern established by Henri IV in 1607 persisted until the Revolution. Royal intervention was felt directly in Paris but also in the provinces. Where Henri IV had built the Place Royale in the east, Louis XIV added the Place Louis-le-Grand (now Place Vendôme) to the west of the old city and Louis XV laid out the Champs Élysées and Place Louis XV (now Place de la Concorde). All were on greenfield sites or on land already in the control of the Crown; for although the Crown had absolute right to expropriate property, there was nevertheless a reluctance to upset the richest landowners (Trintignac 1964). In the provinces, Louis XIV in particular promoted a whole series of developments, either in the form of entirely new settlements, such as Neufbrisach or Montlouis, or in association with port development, as at Brest, Lorient and Sète, or in town extensions, as at Lille or Marseille. In the case of the latter, there was local opposition, but realizing that what the Crown decreed would take place anyway, the municipal authorities in the end agreed and thus ensured that at least the extensions took place under local control (Chartier & Neveux 1981).

The regulatory controls for Paris contained in the edict of 1607 were little by little extended to the whole country. Central control was extended through the *intendants* that Louis XIV had created to represent the Crown in the provinces, and the practice of issuing *permis de construire* became widespread in the eighteenth century. Although the control represented a kind of administrative modernism, the procedure still involved a series of courtly offices and was based on the concept of eminent domain held by the Crown (Le Roy Ladurie 1981). The basic form of control remained the protection of building lines and the use of building materials: a royal decree of 1765 introduced the of a plan for building lines (Bordessoule & Guillemin 1956). During the eighteenth century the growth of towns accelerated, and under Louis XV suburban development, beyond the line of exterior boulevards that had hitherto been rigorously controlled, was encouraged in the form of *lotissements* (subdivisions) that were then built up plot by plot. At the same time an increase in the density of existing fabric took place, by the subdivision of existing plots and by increasing the heights of buildings (Le Roy Ladurie 1981). Control on building heights was not introduced until 1783, with a royal edict that also established a minimum street width (Bastié 1964, Evenson 1979); as Sutcliffe (1970) remarks, this was an important first step in controlling density that had by then become excessive. This height-to-width relationship was established at the very moment it had been abandoned in the 1774 London Building Act.

The Haussmann era

The controls over building lines and the heights of buildings were far too useful to be abandoned at the Revolution and were re-enacted in 1791. Equally significant was the treatment of the issue of expropriation. The Declaration of the Rights of Man had specifically identified the right to property as "inviolable and sacred", in direct opposition to the arbitrary exercise of the royal power to expropriate. The Constitution of the Republic thereafter enshrined that right. Perhaps it was inevitable, however, that a desire to reinstate a power to control and to expropriate should eventually be given effect. The *Code civil* prepared under Napoleon I in 1804 thus substantially qualified this absolute right to enjoy property in two important ways. Article 544 defines property as:

> The right to enjoy and dispose of things in the most absolute manner provided that the usage that is made of them is not prohibited by law or by regulation. (cited by Bergel 1973: 1–2)

The following article prohibits expropriation "unless in the public interest [*pour cause d'utilité publique*] and on condition of prior payment of fair compensation" (cited by Trintignac 1964: 21). Almost from the beginning, therefore, codified law paved the way for continued state intervention in urban development, and the use of the concept of *utilité publique* was to become a staple of modern French planning practice. Further guarantees to owners were introduced in modifications to the law in 1833 and 1841 (Trintignac 1964) and the possibility of expropriation was extended to provincial cities (Roncayolo 1983). The legislative potential for renewed control of the urban environment was thus in place by the beginning of the nineteenth century and was coupled to a revitalized administrative system. On the one hand was the prefectoral system imposed by Napoleon on the territorial divisions of the country created after 1791, the *départements*. On the other were the élite corps of engineers of the Ponts-et-Chaussées who formed the backbone of technical expertise for the country as a whole, and again were allocated by *département*. Yet the problem of densely developed and poorly serviced central Paris remained.

The law on *alignments* passed in 1807 left the initiative to the owner who was only required to conform to the new building lines on demolition. A prohibition on repair was not very effective and tended to lead to the further deterioration of the building stock rather than to redevelopment (Roncayolo 1983). Expropriation, now in principle possible, was hamstrung by being strictly limited to land needed for highways and to be retained in public ownership. The 1841 legislation was created primarily with a view to railway building. Paris in the first half of the nineteenth century was evidently a city that was conspicuous for its lack of domestic comfort, by comparison with London (Olsen 1986). Only in the newer districts beyond the boulevards and between the Champs–Élysées and the Seine was the kind of speculative building taking place that could compare in style or comfort to London developments. Cholera was, as in England, one of the factors that began to concentrate minds. In 1850 expropriation was extended to cover all property on the grounds of insanitary conditions. By this stage, however, we are already on the threshold of the massive intervention undertaken by Haussmann on the orders of Napoleon III.

Louis-Napoleon had come to power after the overthrow of the monarchy in 1848 and was at first President of the Second Republic. By 1851 he had assumed personal power through a *coup d'état* and by 1852 had declared himself emperor. His ambitions for re-establishing the greatness of France in Europe were mirrored in his ambitions for Paris as the imperial capital. Certainly, much needed to be done. The problems of sanitation had hardly been tackled before 1848 and some limited street improvements carried out in the centre of Paris by the prefect Rambuteau in the 1840s was the limit of new work. Napoleon III's inspiration appears paradoxically to have been London. As a young man he had seen the creation of Regent Street and Regent's Park as an example of royal intervention on a grand scale, which had produced an architectural magnificence worthy of a capital (Girouard 1985). The idea of cutting through the old fabric of Paris to create a series of boulevards that would improve circulation, remove slum property and beautify the city was Napoleon III's ambition, although the essentials of his grand plan were not new. Already under Louis XVI the plans for Paris had been prepared, which introduced the concept of the grand cross of east–west and north–south routes, which would relieve congestion both of buildings and of traffic in the centre. Napoleon I had made a start on putting the plan into effect by the creation of the Rue de Rivoli, in 1812. What Napoleon III lacked on the point of proclaiming himself emperor was a person capable of carrying out his proposals. In 1853 he appointed Haussmann, who already had an administrative track record as prefect in Bordeaux, to be prefect of the *département* of Seine to undertake the project.

The transformation of Paris under the guiding hand of Haussmann is now well documented and falls outside the scope of this book (Sutcliffe 1970, Evenson 1979). However, some features of the astonishing speed with which Haussmann changed the face of the city require explanation. The first is the use and development of regulatory controls, which were essential to the success of the project. Indeed, the key legislation had been passed before Haussman's appointment in 1852. The decree of 26 March, which applied to Parisian streets, gave the power to the administration to expropriate land other than that required for the new alignment "for the suppression of former public ways deemed unnecessary" (cited by Roncayolo 1983: 106). It further allowed the administration to judge whether the parcels that remained were adequate for the creation of buildings that met sanitary requirements. If they were judged inadequate, expropriation might be extended to them too. This decree was certainly more extensive than anything that had preceded it and it allowed the authorities to consider levels as well as alignments, and introduced a proper system for *permis de construire*:

> Anyone building a house must henceforward ascertain the alignment and the level of the public way in front of his property and conform to them; he must present a plan and dimensional section of the proposed construction and subject them to the conditions that will be imposed in the interests of public health and safety. (Cited by Trintignac 1964)

These applications for permissions to build were evidently dealt with by the municipal authorities in Bureau de Voirie (Haussmann 1979). Thus, Haussmann had available to him extensive powers to expropriate and extensive powers to regulate the form of new building. However, he did not intend that Paris should be transformed simply by the process of piecemeal redevelopment in conformity with building lines, and the accent from the beginning was on developing new streets rather than relying on the initiative of individual developers. What Haussmann achieved in Paris was attempted elsewhere: indeed most of the major provincial cities emulated Haussmann's approach to urban redevelopment. The prefect of Rhône, Vaïsse, laid out a series of magnificent new thoroughfares in Lyon in a programme of work whose start actually pre-dated Haussmann's appointment. Marseille, Lille and Bordeaux followed suit and then smaller towns such as Orléans, Montpellier and Avignon; as Roncayolo (1983) puts it: "At the other end of the chain the same impulse is to be found in the opening or the projected opening of a Rue Impériale or an Avenue de la Gare or Grand Place", to which even the smallest towns may bear witness. Interestingly, there was a diffusion of technical expertise; thus, Poncet, who had laid out the Rue Impériale (now Rue de la République) at Lyon, went on to projects first at Rouen and then in Nice. Diffusion of the regulatory aspect of the 1852 decree also took place on a rather more limited scale. Article 7 allowed communes in the *département* of Seine to ask for the application of the statute in their area, and 37 did so in the period between 1854 and 1900 (Bastié 1964).

The second feature of the process of the transformation of Paris and the provincial cities was the coming together of public intervention with the interest of the development industry. Speculative pressure had already led to development immediately adjacent to Paris. Olsen (1986) refers to the area of the Chaussée d'Antin, and Sutcliffe (1981) to the suburbs of Grenelle and Batignolles, but these kinds of co-ordinated development were the exception rather than the rule. Haussmann's initiative provided the perfect ground on which a speculative development industry could flourish, and credit was made available to finance the operation. The brothers Péreire, for example, started their involvement in building with one or two major but limited developments, but "little by little extended their activity over the whole surface of Paris" (Halbwachs, cited by Roncayolo 1983: 77). The development industry became geared to the massive intervention of the state and a symbiosis existed between developers, state power and the availability of credit. While the Cubitts were laying out Belgravia and Pimlico and village suburbs on their own initiative in the outskirts of London, Péreire and Poncet were dependent upon the activities and powers of central, and later local, government to proceed in Paris and the provinces. When that symbiosis broke down, as it did in the later nineteenth century under the pressure of financial crises in the 1860s and again in the 1880s, work projected in the Haussmann mould faltered. Local authorities were too weak, and their level of indebtedness as a result of earlier speculations was too great, to complete what they had set in train (Roncayolo 1983). Development in Paris reverted to a pattern that was dictated by the dispersal of property ownership.

Suburban development and the creation of the lotissements

The Haussmann model was thus predicated on the involvement of public authorities creating new streets in the public interest, which stimulated private activity, which in turn could then be controlled through regulation. In the suburbs the story was rather different. Haussmann, although prefect of the whole of the *département* of Seine, was not interested in street improvement outside the limits of Paris, albeit enlarged to its present size by Napoleon III. Beyond, the rapidly suburbanizing communes on the periphery saw little in the way of public interest in creating new streets, and the property industry by and large saw no potential away from the boulevards. The communes of the Parisian suburbs increasingly sought application of the regulatory control offered by the 1852 decree, and regulations allowed them to fix standards for new roads if they were adopted and maintained by the municipal authorities. A failure to respect these standards in principle resulted in new roads being considered private and liable to closure. In practical terms, however, municipal resources were not equal to the task, and development was often incoherent and under-serviced, because the small developers who carried out the work by and large lacked the skills in land assembly and road layout.

There were of course exceptions. Apart from the developments already noted on the edge of the then built-up areas of Paris in the 1830s and 1840s, examples of planned layouts undertaken by speculators are to be found. Le Vésinet was laid out as an integrated villa suburb in 1848, capitalizing on the access offered by the newly completed Paris–St-Germain railway. Belleville, although within the confines of Paris after 1852, was not subject to Haussmann's attention and developed largely at the hands of speculators, some of whom in the late nineteenth century were able to assembly "several tens of thousands of square metres of land" (Roncayolo 1983: 122). On an even larger scale was the creation of the suburb of Levallois–Perret from 1845 by the developer Levallois, who evidently laid out the simple grid pattern of streets and organized the letting of sites and gathering together of building tradesmen. Such was his success that his "new town" was created an independent commune in 1866, bearing his name. But, whether on the scale of Levallois or at a more modest level, there was a clear distinction between site developers and ultimate builders. Land was let off in small parcels to individuals, whether professional builders or future owner-occupiers to develop (Roncayolo 1983). If the Parisian suburbs did see some involvement of professionals, elsewhere the output was even more haphazard. Bonneville (1979), in his study of Villeurbanne, emphasizes the role of traditional farm buildings and self-built accommodation in the housing of this working-class suburb of Lyon, which developed rapidly in the second half of the nineteenth century.

The concept of the *lotissement* (subdivision), in which land was sold to individuals, was indeed well developed by the end of the nineteenth century, even if its notoriety did not reach a peak until the 1920s and 1930s. Encircling Paris were a series of large landholdings that had originally been either monastic or aristocratic and had become by the nineteenth century rural retreats for the wealthy middle class. From the middle of the century, landowners increasingly sought their pleasures elsewhere and the outward expansion of Paris began to create a hope value where none had hitherto existed, given the poor yields in forestry, to which much of the land was given over. The very first example of a *lotissement* was, according Bergel (1973: 25), the development of what had been Boileau's estate by the Lemercier at Auteuil from 1839, where purchasers were limited to building "*maisons de campagne*". Early examples of subdivisions for *pavillons à jardinets* (villas with gardens) (Bastié 1964: 202) occur first at Romainville in 1848 and in the next decade at Bois–Colombes, Pavillons-sous-Bois, Le Raincy and Villemomble, all on forested land.

Until 1914 this development excited little comment and few of the subdivisions were defective in their servicing or layout. The subdivisions were generally small and, according to Bastié, by 1919 less than 3000 ha had been so developed. By 1929 that figure had more than tripled in the suburbs of Paris, and examples were also to be found in the provinces. The reasons for this enormous explosion are not hard to find. The First World War led to a reduction in the number of houses available, an increase in demand and a diversion of resources to reconstruction in the liberated areas. For those trying to find accommodation in Paris, the choice was between an expensive and over-crowded rented room in the centre or a *pavillon* on a subdivision in the outskirts. Given that, unlike the pre-war developments, the *lotissements* of the 1920s were being created for a clientele that had difficulty in paying for a plot, let alone for a building, the lack of servicing is hardly surprising and it rapidly became a scandal. Water and sewerage were for the most part absent on individual plots, and some *lotissements* even lacked a proper system of roads. On plots created, owners built for themselves shacks that rapidly became semi-rural slums, even if later they were consolidated by more substantial construction.

The contrast between the Haussmann model in the central areas of the major cities and the disorganized growth of the lotissements could not be more stark. The communes of the *départements* of Seine, Seine-et-Oise and Seine-et-Marne most affected by the new development lacked both the most rudimentary controls and the financial means to take action. Most communes were simply overwhelmed by the scale of the problem and could do nothing to stop the phenomenon or to regulate it after the event. Indeed, the success of the Haussmann developments in Paris, which relied on public intervention coupled with stringent regulatory controls on building lines and heights, seems to have blinkered the authorities of the Third Republic to more general problems of planning and alternative means of control. The years from 1870 to 1914 saw an extension to the powers of control over building lines, but nothing similar to the development of the regulatory approaches adopted in Britain in the 1849 and 1875 Public Health Acts or in the 1909 Housing and Town Planning etc. Act, far less the systematic town extensions of Germany in the period. The developments in regulatory control that did take place in the period up to 1914 consisted first of a requirement in the municipal law of 1884 that all communes prepare a *plan d'alignement et de nivellement* (plan of building lines and levels) on the model of the regulations in force for Paris (Trintignac 1964). To this was then added the generalized requirement enacted in a statute of 1902 on public heath, to obtain a *permis de construire* that applied to communes with populations of 20000 or more (Bastié 1964), but which according to Trintignac (1964: 32) was "without effect in a certain number of communes". Sutcliffe's (1981) characterization of France as the "reluctant planner" in this period is apt.

The first planning legislation

Nevertheless, the pressures to extend both plan-making and control in this period were growing, and both internal and external influences were beginning to shape a system of planning. As in Britain, the experience of German town extension schemes with their pattern of zoning was an important source of ideas; so too, it would appear, were the zoning plans of the USA, with their rather different set of assumptions (Gaudin 1985). But the move towards a system of plans that would zone uses was also being generated by internal forces. Even under the Haussmann model, use of extended areas of expropriated land in the *alignements en profondeur*, and the increasing differentiation of streets in terms of their function and the classes of buildings that were permitted, pointed in the direction of zoning. As Gaudin observes, it was a short step to apply to the neighbourhood as a whole what had been initially limited to the street. Another influence was that of Tony Garnier's *cité industrielle* project, which offered a model of rigid separation of residential, industrial and commercial quarters, and which was claimed by Le Corbusier as the forerunner of his own ideas on city planning (Mariani 1990).

Choay (1982) argues that a final influence was the experience of colonial planning in Morocco, where Lyautey created town extensions in which there was clear functional separation.

Gaudin points to the reasons why zoning should have been attractive to those concerned with the possibilities for town planning. At one level, it fitted with a "scientific" approach to urban analysis that compartmented the urban fabric according to statistical information gathered. A method that was applied to existing urban areas could easily be extended to planning for the new. More than that, zoning came to be seen as "the vector of a potential return to order in towns that was as much symbolic as practical" (Gaudin 1982: 64). Gaudin argues that zoning served another purpose, too. By identifying actual and potential uses, a zoning plan would underwrite the interests of small landowners, a class who were particularly to the fore in the years of the Third Republic and to whom the Commune of 1871 that had opened the period had been potentially threatening.

The Loi Cornudet

The pressures of urbanization and the existence of an increasingly influential body of people concerned to promote *urbanisme* – the term was coined apparently in 1912 (Choay 1982) – led to the comprehensive legislation in 1919 that is known as the Loi Cornudet. It did not emerge unheralded. There had been three attempts to enact comprehensive planning legislation in the years between 1900 and 1914 (Trintignac 1964), and the 1919 legislation showed little development from the first of its three predecessors (Sutcliffe 1981). The law required that all communes with a population greater than 10000 should prepare a *projet d'aménagement*, which would consist of a *plan d'aménagement, d'embellissement et d'extension* identifying buildings in the public interest, open spaces, a future road network, and zonings for residential and industrial development (Bordessoule & Guillemin 1956). In addition to the plan, the *projet* was to contain a series of building regulations (Besson 1971). Finally, the use of the *permis de construire* delivered by the mayor became obligatory in all communes required to have a plan, while *lotissements* required special authorization from the prefect. In addition to these general requirements, the law was also applied to all communes in the Seine *département* and to all communes experiencing rapid growth or having particular architectural character (Bordessoule & Guillemin 1956, Bastié 1964).

Wide-ranging powers they may have been, but totally ineffective in practice. The period between 1919 and 1924 witnessed some of the worst excesses of *lotissement* development in the Parisian suburbs. Moreover, the requirement to prepare plans within three years was not enforced (Besson 1971). The more or less total failure of the Loi Cornudet led to further legislation in 1924, which made good some, but not all, of the omissions of the earlier legislation. The principal weakness seemed to be the failure of central government to make available the necessary financial and technical resources with which the communes could

51

implement legislation. By 1939, of 1938 communes required by the statute to prepare a plan, only 273 had an approved plan in force and a further 158 had a plan in preparation (Bordessoule & Guillemin 1956). Nevertheless, some important principles were established in 1919. In particular, the three-way relationship between a plan with zones for different activities, a series of regulations for construction and a requirement to seek a permission to build dates from this period. The laws of 1919 and 1924 also confirmed that plan-making and development control would essentially be undertaken at communal level, albeit under the watchful eye of the central administration.

Although the problem of controlling the *lotissements* had been more or less solved by 1939, the more general question of plan-making and control had still not effectively been dealt with. The next important step forwards took place during the war years and was the work of the Vichy government in 1943. In some ways the 1943 statute represented a clear line of descent from the legislation of 1919 and 1924: it retained the same relationship within a *plan d'aménagement*, regulations and *permis de construire*. Communes with populations greater than 10000 were once again required to prepare a plan. The section dealing with *permis de construire* now brought together into a single process three separate types of permission and extended the obligation to seek permission to the country as a whole (Bordessoule & Guillemin 1956, Piron 1994). However, there were some important breaks with previous practice, which mainly had to do with the administration for planning. To enhance control by the centre, a Délégation Générale à l'Équipement National was set in place at national level with representation in the regions and the *départements*. Plan-making would be carried out at the expense of the state by an appropriate professional named by the mayor with the approval of central government, and the plan would be approved by the Conseil d'État. *Permis de construire* were for the most part to be issued by the prefect. In part this move away from local to central control was a direct reflection of the centralizing and authoritarian tendencies of the régime. In part, however, it reflected concern for the weaknesses of the Loi Cornudet. The inadequacy of funding and the lack of technical resources available to most communes was seen as a major contributory factor in the failure of integrated planning, as was the lack of steer from central government.

Nevertheless, there is an apparent paradox in the fact that legislation passed at the height of the collaboration with Nazi Germany should have been re-enacted after the Liberation and have held the same kind of relationship to current French practice, as the 1947 Town and Country Planning Act does to current British practice. The explanation is twofold. On the one hand there was a continuity in the personnel involved with both pre- and post-war planning. In particular, Piron (1994) notes that Prothin, who was Director of Planning under Laval, took the precaution of consulting the Free French in London before presenting the Bill to the Vichy Government, and was to remain in post until 1958. On the other hand, the 1943 law clearly represented a continuity of thinking about the nature of plan-making and control, and the question of appropriate levels of administration that transcended the upheavals of the war years. The 1943 statute did not merely make good the deficiencies of the earlier legislation; it integrated the powers and procedures for planning into the mainstream of French governance. For the time, the term *urbanisme* acquired a legal significance and the provisions of plan-making and control were properly codified (Besson 1971). The form of French development control as it was to emerge after 1945 is thus firmly rooted in the conception of government, to which we need now to turn.

The administrative context for the control of development

To understand the conception of government that informs the French system of planning, we need to return to the events of the French Revolution. So far, the history of the control of development has been presented as a continuum that straddled easily the tumult of the late eighteenth century. Certainly, too, the centralization of French administration that is one remarkable feature of the nineteenth and twentieth centuries had already been set in train by the Bourbon monarchs. The Revolution did nevertheless have a profound impact on the internal government of France, such that most of the structures, the relationships and the tensions that now exist within French administration can be traced back to the immediate aftermath of the Revolution.

Commentators not infrequently point to the chaos that characterized French local administration under the *ancien régime* (for example, Legendre 1964). Although there had been some attempt at uniform control by the creation of the *intendances* under Louis XIV, there were also a whole series of *bailliages* and *sénéchaussées* and other administrative divisions, each with their own status, rights and privileges, and, although some of the provinces had provincial assemblies, as many did not. To that diversity of administration must be added a more general diversity in the French population. Most French citizens, for example, did not speak French as a first language in 1789; apparently, nearly a quarter of the population did not speak it at all (Rickard 1989). The guarantee of national cohesion was provided by the institution of the monarchy as expressed in the person of the king: you were French because you owed allegiance to the French monarch. Thus, to abolish the monarchy was to create an acute crisis in governance that required an immediate response if centrifugal forces were not to tear the country apart. The unity of the state became an overriding preoccupation.

The response manifested itself in two ways. The first was to create the state as a legal entity with a written constitution that legitimized all subsequent legislation. The opening words of the Constitution that have endured unchanged in the Fifth Republic underline the central concern: "The French Republic is one and indivisible . . .". The second was to address the problem of administration by providing a form of internal government that was rational and egalitarian, and, by so doing, replace with a sense of French citizenhood the provincial loyalties that were threatening in the absence of the monarchy. The old provinces

53

were thus abandoned in favour of structure of 90 (now 96) *départements*, which took their names from geographical features. The theory on which these *départements* were created was that every citizen would be within a day's ride of the administrative capital. In the event, the subdivision of the country was not quite the *tabula rasa* that it might appear. In practice, provincial boundaries were often respected, even if the provinces themselves were subdivided and the names abandoned. In some cases a new *département* corresponded more or less exactly to an older unit. Thus, the Comté de Foix become the *département* of Ariège, and modern Dordogne retained the boundaries of ancient Périgord (François 1976).

Over the course of the next 100 years, this structure of *départements* was then fleshed out with a pattern of administration that was designed to guarantee the unity of France. Indeed, it would be wiser to talk of administrations in the plural (Machin 1979). Some of the major innovations were Napoleonic. Napoleon was responsible for the prefectoral system that placed a representative of central government, the *préfet* (prefect), in each of the *départements*. The prefect was there both to transmit imperial orders and to be a source of information for the centre. There was, moreover, underneath the prefect a hierarchy of state representatives in the form of the sub-prefects with the responsibility for an *arrondissement*, and at the lowest level, the local mayor. Napoleon also set in place a second form of administration that has endured to the present day, in the form of the ministerial field services. This was designed to create a comprehensive network of technical experts in each of the *départements*. Foremost among these experts were the engineers of the Ponts-et-Chaussées who have made a major impact in providing the country with modern infrastructure. Nominally, these technical services were responsible to the prefect, although in practice they have tended to be controlled by their ministries in Paris, and in the event have often enjoyed considerable freedom of action.

To control the activities of both his new administration and the population at large, Napoleon created a series of legal codes that spelt out the rights, duties and responsibilities of administrator and *administré* alike. The law thus not only defines the state, it also controls the state's behaviour and provides the rules by which state and citizens conduct their lives and interact with each other. Codified administrative law is thus predicated on the concept of abolishing the arbitrariness of royal power and replacing it with the certainty of the rule of law and the possibility of redress in the event of grievance. Codified administrative law thus enters deeply into daily life. Paradoxically, in spite of its totalitarian origins, it is a system that has come to be a guarantor of third-party rights without equal (Weil 1965). And in the politically unstable climate of the nineteenth century, the role of administrative law was paramount in ensuring continuity of the administration and enhancing its status (Brown & Bell 1993).

Within any discussion of administrative law, reference needs to be made to the Conseil d'État. Yet another creation of Napoleon I, the prime function of the Conseil d'État was to advise government on the drafting of new laws and regulations, but it also acted as a court of appeal in the case of a dispute between a citizen and the administration. The judicial role of the Conseil d'État thus became increasingly important in the nineteenth century and was confirmed by its creation as an independent court under the Third Republic. After the Second World War, the volume of judicial work handled by the Conseil d'État became so great that 26 (later reduced to 24) *tribunaux administratifs* (administrative courts) were established to deal with the great body of the work, leaving the Conseil d'État to act as a court of last appeal.

However, there was another preoccupation of the leaders of the Revolution that was to have an equally profound effect on present administration. The perceived need was to create an administration that would transmit the ideals of liberty, equality and fraternity to the populace at large and to foster the principle of democratic government at the most local level. Although the 1790s saw prolonged debate on the right form of local government, the solution advanced by Thouret was essentially pragmatic. If the population at large were to be engaged in a democratic process, it was essential that democracy came to structures with which people were familiar. Hence, the decision was taken to use the parishes of the *ancien régime*, renamed communes, as the training ground for democracy. These communes would in principle be free to administer themselves within the framework of the law (Bourjol 1975, Winock 1989). A system of locally elected municipal councils was created for the communes under the Third Republic, as were councils for each of the *départements*. However, in spite of the intentions of the Revolution, the extent of communal freedom to act has always been an issue, with the central state seeking at various times to limit communes' powers and always concerned to regulate their activities. The remarkable thing is the way that on each occasion when the central state has sought to concentrate power, the interests of the communes have been as vigorously defended, as a bulwark against totalitarianism. Thus, the 40 000 parishes of the *ancien régime* have resisted, in the face of all attempts at amalgamation, becoming the 36 551 communes of contemporary metropolitan France.

This is the framework that gave rise to the 1943 planning legislation. The codification of planning law and regulations, formalized in the publication in 1954 of the first *Code de l'urbanisme et de l'habitation*, marks the entry of planning control into the administrative mechanisms of the state. The code allows the citizen to know his or her rights and the administration its obligations. Through the code the administration may be held to account. It is important to recognize that the *plans d'aménagement* and the system of granting *permis de construire* were a central element within this codified framework. Thus, the plans and their regulations were to be understood as local extensions of the generalized provisions of the code, identifying the albeit highly circumscribed rights of landowners and developers. By the same token, the code and the regulations attached to the plans provided the sole criteria by which permissions to build could be judged. Plans became legalized documents that could be challenged in the court. Control decisions could be contested by reference to the appropriate regulations. Zoning provided a perfect vehicle for conveying the spatial distribution of those rights and duties.

The evolution of planning control also fits into the evolution of the administration. Haussmann operated as prefect of the *département* of Seine at a time when central control was paramount, but even he found it politic to work with the city council of Paris, even though council members were appointed and not elected. Haussmann nonetheless represented the kind of technocratic control of planning that has continued to the present day. On the other hand, as an antidote to the centralized control of Napoleon III, the Third Republic favoured the democratization of local government. Thus, in 1884 it was specifically the communes that were charged with the preparation of *plans d'alignement*, and in 1919 the powers to make plans and issue *permis de construire* were given to mayors of communes. Herein, of course, lay one of the essential weaknesses of the Loi Cornudet. The vast majority of communes were far too small to envisage planning work, lacking both the financial and technical resources to take the necessary action. When communes did act, the plans they produced were still subject to approval by the Conseil d'État, it is true. This afforded a measure of central control and guaranteed the legality of the plans produced, but it also made the process cumbersome, and was perhaps another reason for the failure of the Loi Cornudet.

Planning control in the Fourth Republic

The key administrative issues to be resolved, then, were the relationship between central and local control and the availability of technical expertise. For the Vichy government, unlike the Third Republic, the main concern was indeed to assert a greater degree of central control over the country. That they chose to do so, by putting a new system of technical control in place, accorded well both with the preoccupations of those concerned with planning, but who were not in favour of Vichy authoritarianism, and with an existing pattern of administration. The 1943 act set up the Délégation Générale à l'Équipement National as the main source of technocratic centralized control for planning. In fact, the Délégation had existed since 1941 with a specific remit of preparing for post-war reconstruction (Trintignac 1964, Piron 1994). The 1943 Act further concentrated this technocratic control by providing for regional and departmental field services on the Napoleonic model. After 1945, the Délégation became a ministry in its own right and the field services were retained to become the Directions Départementales de l'Équipement (*DDE*) whose role in post-war planning in France has been crucial. The 1943 legislation survived the Liberation because it responded to concerns that were wider than those of the Vichy government.

The innovations of the 1943 legislation and their survival into the Fourth Republic highlights an issue that was to become central to the debate over the following 50 years, on both planning and local administration. As Bordessoule & Guillemin (1956: 14) put it:

- should the Ministry be primarily a body concerned to coordinate and give a stimulus with the implementation of programmes devised under its general control being left to local authorities?

- or should it, carry out directly and more or less completely the implementation of urban policy and regional development, with the risk of the reduction in local freedoms that that implies?

After the Liberation, the government acted immediately to extend planning laws to the whole of the country by order of the administration in June 1945. The following October, mindful of the need to restore democratic control at a local level, the mayor replaced the prefect as the decision-maker on *permis de construire* in most cases, although he or she did so as agent of the state, not as locally elected representative. On the other hand, the powers to approve *lotissements*, which had also been transferred to the prefect in 1943, were not reverted in 1945. Thus, as Besson (1971) observes, the post-war regime on *lotissements* was markedly more authoritarian than its pre-war predecessors. Moreover, this had the effect of aligning the procedures for *lotissements* in what the French call operational planning, rather than seeing them as a reactive control. Both Besson and Bordessoule & Guillemin note that the effect of generalizing the planning system was to give the administration very wide powers, and in particular wide discretion to the prefect. It is especially worth noting that Parliament itself did not legislate as far as *permis de construire* are concerned: until 1967 the procedures were laid down by government decree, not by primary legislation, which explains in part the power that the central administration acquired.

The significant problems of the post-war regime for *permis de construire* were not simply those of central versus local control, important though they were. In spite of the generalizing and unifying of the procedures in 1945, a very serious deficiency remained in plan-making. For all that there was now in principle a system of zoning plans, coverage of the country remained sparse, with an obligation to prepare being limited to communes with populations greater than 10000. Moreover, in spite of the existence of an administration capable of delivering technical support, plans still required the approval of the Conseil d'État. Where plans were made, the regulations attaching to them were "all too often . . . ill-assorted and insufficient, relating to public health or building lines" (Labetoulle 1982: 10). In the rest of the country the only grounds that could be used for refusing an application were public health regulations of the *département* or of the commune. The regulations thus provided only the most schematic basis for the streamlined system of control, and this at the very moment that economic development and population growth were leading to unprecedented pressures on land development. Permissions granted for new building increased from 38000 in 1948 to nearly 175000 by 1954 (Bordessoule & Guillemin 1956: 75), and it is perhaps hardly surprising that the refusal rate was a mere 1.8 per cent in 1954, having dropped from 5 per cent in 1951.

To remedy this lack of a proper regulatory base, a new decree in 1955 pro-

duced a series of *règles nationales d'urbanisme* (RNU: national planning regulations) that would apply to the country as a whole. They were designed to extend
the scope of control and to ensure consistency and fairness in the granting of permissions. But it was a system that in remedying one set of defects merely created
others. In one way the existence of national regulations merely highlighted the
inadequacy of local planning. Regulations applicable across the country as a
whole could in no sense be said to represent planning policies, although, as with
other normative controls, there was a strategic objective implicit in the exercise
of tactical decision-making. Moreover, there was the added difficulty of determining which rules should apply in a given case. Finally, the most difficult issue
had to do with the inflexibility of regulations in the face of the rapid growth that
post-war France experienced; as Labetoulle puts it:

> . . . the ideal rule of law is one which anticipates, foresees, organizes and
> channels urban development; and when data on urban development are rap-
> idly and frequently called into question, the rule of law, by nature inflexible,
> finds itself overshadowed" (1982: 11).

The strategies to deal with this problem were equally problematic. On the one
hand, where the regulations appeared too constraining, the administration
required a discretion to depart from the regulation in force in the event; on the
other, there was another discretion to postpone the decision in the light of rules
not yet in force. Such discretionary power was to prove enormously contentious.
It offended against the basic principle of clarity, certainty and fairness that a codified system of administrative law was supposed to confer. Where was the justice
if a rule could be waived in one instance but upheld in another? Secondly, to
those who supported local democracy, such discretion was seen as allowing the
central administration an unacceptably large and unaccountable power of decision-making that led to collusion and compromise. If, as Labetoulle (1982: 12)
claims, abuse was not widespread, particular instances nevertheless gave sufficient grounds to sustain this objection.

Reform: refining the control system

These difficulties with the unified system of development control were not much
affected by two important changes to the law, in the form of a new system of
plans in 1958 and modifications to the RNU in 1962. Of the two, by far the most
significant was the new system of plans. The old *plans d'aménagement* were converted into two sorts of *plan d'urbanisme*. The *plan d'urbanisme directeur* was
required to divide into zones the land to which it applied, as well as to indicate
new road lines, public open spaces and land for public purposes. The *plan d'urbanisme de détail* was an essentially analogous document, but instead of applying to
a whole commune or to a group of communes, was prepared for a part of a commune where development or rapid change was envisaged. Once again, both types

of plan were required only for communes of 10000 inhabitants or more. Nevertheless, some progress seems to have been made with plan-making, as 5000 plans were created jointly under the 1943 and 1958 legislation (Jégouzo & Pittard 1980: 36). 1958 also saw the introduction of an instrument that was seen as the hallmark of interventionist operational planning in the form of the *zone à urbaniser en priorité* (ZUP: priority development zone). It was a mechanism that was designed for the creation of peripheral high-rise housing estates, which by the 1990s had come to be seen as the seat of urban social malaise. Within the zone, it was possible to concentrate the provision of public services in a way that was cost-effective.

The 1958 system of plans was modified again in the Loi d'Orientation Foncière of 1967 that set up the system that is now current. A two-tier hierarchy of plans was maintained, but instead of two types of plan being similar in form and effect, a clear distinction was made between strategic and detailed local planning. At the local level, the *plan d'urbanisme de détail* was replaced by the *plan d'occupation des sols* (POS: local land-use plan) that was to be a zoning document with accompanying regulations. Although there were some important differences in detail and in procedure, and the obligation to prepare a POS was extended, POS followed closely in a line of development from the earlier plans. They would be prepared normally for a single commune (although they have sometimes been used to cover several) and the procedure by which they were prepared was to be one of partnership between the state and the communes concerned, with the mayor in principle taking an important role (Chapuisat 1983). The upper tier of plans was a distinct break with previous practice. The *schéma directeur d'aménagement et d'urbanisme* (SD: strategic development plan) would provide a strategic base to which the POS would conform, but were not themselves binding on landowners and developers in the way that the POS were. Two points are worth making at this stage. The first is that, whereas the implicit intention of the 1967 legislation was that the country would eventually be covered by POS to provide a local regulatory framework for all development control decisions, there was no such intention for SD. The second is that making the SD a document that could not be directly applied to decisions on *permis de construire* led inevitably to a legal challenge through the courts, when, for example, a POS did not conform to a SD.

The 1967 legislation did not radically change the system for *permis de construire,* although there was one important innovation. This was to remove the requirement that the project had to conform to the *règles générales de construction* (general building regulations) in favour of an undertaking that the regulations would be respected. Thus, the *permis de construire* became more closely a planning than a building control.

In spite of the implicit intention to achieve universal coverage, progress with POS was slow in the 1970s. In part, the lack of progress was attributable to the fact that older-style plans were allowed to continue in force until 1975, a period that was extended until 1978. The final abandonment of the *plans d'urbanisme* of the 1958 legislation led to an upsurge in POS preparation, and by 1980 work on plan preparation was at a substantially higher level than at any time previously

59

(Labetoulle 1982). Although much of the country's population lived in areas in which *POS* were approved or in preparation, still only a third of all communes were involved. For those communes without a plan, the *RNU* continued to provide the regulatory base for decisions on *permis de construire*. Indeed, the *RNU* continued to be improved in parallel to the improvements to the system of plans. At the same time that refinements were being made to the *POS* in 1977, the *RNU* was being extended to cover certain environmental concerns such as nature conservation and noise nuisance.

A final innovation in 1967 was the *zone d'aménagement concerté* (*ZAC*: concerted development zone), which was to replace the *ZUP*. *ZUP* had been limited to the development of large-scale public sector estates. The *ZAC* was conceived to deal with either public or private sector development and all types of land use. It was to be used where development was to be encouraged and it spelt out in detail how such development would be carried out. In simple *ZAC* the regulations of the *POS* would often be sufficient to provide the regulatory framework. Where the proposed development was more complex, the *ZAC* would carry its own plan of regulations that replaced the *POS*. Crucially, however, in either case, the *ZAC* created a framework for agreement on providing service infrastructure.

Decentralization of planning powers

Thus, by the early 1980s France had a fully articulated system for the control of development, which in effect consisted of two parallel streams. Where there was a *POS* the *permis de construire* was evaluated in relation to the regulations of the *POS*, which covered more or less the entire criteria for a decision. Where there was no *POS*, the *RNU*, by now much extended, formed the basis of decision-making. At this point we need to consider the system for controlling development in the light of administrative reform and in particular the decentralization of powers to local authorities that was initiated during Mitterrand's first term of office, in 1982.

The syndicat de communes

By the 1970s, the tension between the desire to maintain the unity of the state through centralized control and the deeply held belief in the value of the commune as the basic unit of democracy was in urgent need of resolution. There were several dimensions to the problem. Most communes were far too small to be effective providers of services on their own and had long since formed partnerships with their neighbours to deal with, among other things, water, sewage disposal and garbage collection. Finding an appropriate level for developing coherent planning policies for the larger urban areas was equally pressing. At another level, there was grave resentment at what was often seen as the heavy hand of central intervention in local affairs, not least in planning. The larger cities, in particular, wished to be free of the constraint, because they had both the political will and the necessary resources to achieve the independence that was largely denied them.

However, attempts at reform and calls for decentralization are not a recent phenomenon. The problem is that reform has been proposed for a variety of motives. Gourevitch (1980), for example, notes that whereas some reforms have been intended to increase local autonomy, others have had to do with a desire for increased rationality and efficiency, and yet others were designed to increase, not to loosen, central control. Of the many different attempts at reform, there are three that centrally concern us in relation to the control of development.

The first and oldest of these are the possibilities that exist for communes to form *syndicats* (syndical groupings) with their neighbours for the delivery of services. The *syndicat* was effectively a way out of the flat refusal of communes to submit to amalgamation, which in any case had suffered from the taint of authoritarianism, in that it was the favoured solution of the Vichy regime (Bourjol 1975). First introduced in 1890, the *syndicat* overcame the limitations of small communes, without the communes themselves having to give up any of their rights and privileges. The post-war period saw the principle of the *syndicat* reinforced in two stages. Legislation in 1959 amended the rules and led to arrangements for *syndicats intercommunaux à vocation unique* (*SIVU*: single-purpose syndicates) and *syndicats intercommunaux à vocation multiple* (*SIVOM*: multipurpose syndicates). The former were to be syndicates to deliver a single service, the latter, as the name suggests, where several services were to be provided jointly. Communes in these syndicates would agree which services would be provided in common and would vote funds to be managed by a committee of delegates. The 1959 legislation also made possible a grouping known as the *district*, conceived primarily for urban areas. Some activities of the districts were prescribed by law; others were to be added by delegation from the communes. Once again the district was managed by a council of delegates. The chief distinction of the districts, other than its duties prescribed by law, was the ability to raise its own taxes (Maurice 1976, Richard & Cotten 1986).

The final form of grouping introduced in 1966 was the *communauté urbaine* (urban community). The intention was to create an effective means for governing the major conurbations, which were mainly split between large numbers of communes. As with the districts, the duties of *communautés urbaines* were prescribed by law, although the list was considerably longer than that for districts. For the first time, urban planning and plan preparation were a requirement, although not the control of development through the processing of applications for *permis de construire*. *Communautés urbaines* were also empowered to raise taxes on property, employment and residence, in effect as a precept on the taxes raised by individual communes. They were also able to receive part of the income tax generated by the population within their areas. Four of these *communautés urbaines* were brought into existence by central government, in an attempt to stop central city communes such as Lyon going their own way: the four conurbations that had *communautés urbaines* imposed upon them were Bordeaux, Lille, Lyon and Strasbourg. A further five *communautés urbaines* were created voluntarily (Maurice 1976).

These forms of grouping have worked precisely because of their voluntarist nature and, of the four forms of grouping, the *SIVOM* or the *SIVU* have been by far the most widely used, because they require that the constituent communes relinquish least of their autonomy. Only *communautés urbaines* were ever imposed on communes and the experience is said to have convinced the government that coercion would never work.

The second major reform stems from the same legislation as created the *communautés urbaines*. Concerned to create a proper series of mechanisms for urban planning, De Gaulle created a new Ministère de l'Équipement (Ministry of Infrastructure), which brought together the hitherto separate ministries for construction and highways. This new super-ministry was responsible for the combined field services at departmental level of the Directions Départementales de l'Équipement (*DDE*), whose role in planning has been paramount in the previous 25 years. There appear to have been two motives behind this reform. One was to shift power away from engineers who had traditionally held sway, in favour of a newer breed of planners whose training was in architecture or in the social sciences. The other was to reinforce central control, both by creating a strong technocratic base and, paradoxically, by devolving decision-making power to the *DDE* (Sorbets 1979, Thoenig 1979). Local authorities gained nothing from this shift in the way of freedom to act.

The desire for local control and the Loi Defferre

The concern for the efficiency of local administration has been matched since 1970 by concern for increasing the autonomy of local government. Already in the 1970s Giscard d'Estaing had been persuaded to review local government. The product of this review, the Guichard Report produced in 1976, advocated a coherent structure of communal groupings to which power would be devolved (Guichard 1976). In spite of insisting on the value of the commune as the base unit of local democracy in France, the loss of communal power implied was such as to make the report's findings unacceptable. Mitterrand came to power in 1981 with decentralization as a key objective, but with a very different agenda for its implementation (Gourevitch 1980, Gontcharoff & Milano 1985). The chief architect of the decentralization was Gaston Defferre, then Mayor of Marseille and Mitterrand's Minister for the Interior. As a mayor of a large and powerful commune, it was hardly surprising that, rather than emphasizing the need for rationality and efficiency by seeking new groupings or amalgamations of communes, his major concern was for democracy within the commune. To achieve this, Defferre introduced legislation in three stages. In the first, the statute of 2 March

1982 that became known as the Loi Defferre, the rights and privileges of communes, *départements* and regions were affirmed, with each having a democratically elected council and constituted to administer their activities freely without hierarchical control. Within this new system, prefects changed their role from that of initiator to that of "long-stop", required only to ensure the legality of decisions once taken (the *contrôle de légalité*). The second stage of the legislation in 1983 was to transfer to those freely constituted units of local authority a series of powers and responsibilities. The third, in 1985, concerned the transfer of resources (Flockton 1983, Gontcharoff & Milano 1985).

The significance of decentralization for present purposes is the extent to which urban planning and the control of development were key elements in the powers transferred in 1983. First, communes were now free to decide if and when a *POS* was prepared and could choose the agency to prepare it. Secondly, once a *POS* had been in force for six months, communes were free to determine their own *permis de construire* and to choose the technical agency to process applications. However, in recognition of the limited resources available to communes, the government made the *DDE* available free of charge to communes, both for plan-making and for the processing of *permis de construire*. The prefect was to exercise *contrôle de légalité* in all decisions taken, and to ensure that the state's interests were accommodated in the plans produced. A final power of the 1983 legislation was to limit new development to the existing built-up areas of communes where no *POS* was in force, a provision that became generally known as the *règle de constructibilité limitée* (limited development rule).

Several observations can be made about this transfer of power. First, government was clearly concerned not merely to decentralize planning powers but to encourage plan preparation. Hence, communes were provided both with the incentive to prepare plans – the transfer of the power to determine applications – and a threat if they did not – the limitation on new development. Secondly, government was clearly intent on setting boundaries to communal discretion. By requiring that communes had a *POS* before it was free to process its *permis de construire,* the state ensured that communes would be bound by particularized regulations. By instituting a *contrôle de légalité,* the prefects could verify that the regulations had indeed been respected. By providing the *DDE* free of charge to communes, the state ensured a degree of continuity in the technical input into plans. The central concern in all these limitations appears to have been that the rule of law and the unity of the state were not threatened by the increased freedoms given to communes.

Inevitably, the commentaries that followed questioned whether this decentralization of planning powers could ever be effective. Some commentators saw the state taking back with the left hand what it had given with the right. The prefect's role in the *contrôle de légalité* looked almost as formidable as the powers it had replaced. The presence of the *DDE* was correctly seen as ensuring the continuity of technocratic surveillance. Some critics foresaw that decentralization would work to the benefit of large urban communes, which had the resources and knowledge to break free from state control, leaving a growing divide between them and small suburban and rural communes, which had neither. Yet other critics foresaw that the slowness of preparing *POS* in the 1970s meant that it would take years for all communes to be covered by approved plans and thus achieve control over their own planning destiny. Finally, there was doubt as to whether all communes would wish to take on these new responsibilities (Wilson 1988).

None of these criticisms was without foundation. Yet the balance after 11 years is by no means one of failure. The number of communes with approved or published *POS* had risen from 6400 in 1983 to 13700 in mid-1991 (Ministère de l'Urbanisme, du Logement et des Transports 1985, Ministère de l'Équipement, du Logement, des Transports et de la Mer 1991). This is an enviable record of achievement, which to some extent confounds the critics, particularly since plan coverage now accounts for over 80 per cent of the total population of metropolitan France. On the other hand over 60 per cent of all communes still lack a plan in force and there is clear evidence that starts on the preparation of new plans have fallen markedly since an initial upsurge in the period immediately after decentralization (Priet 1992, Booth 1994), suggesting that there may be an irreducible minimum number of communes that will never prepare a *POS* and thus never acquire decentralized planning powers. For the most part, communes inevitably favoured *DDE* both for plan preparation and for processing applications for *permis de construire*. A mere 5 per cent of communes with *POS* processed their own applications by 1992 (Priet 1992).

The final stage in the process of administrative reform was reached in 1992. The Loi Defferre had deliberately transferred powers to the units of local authority as they then existed. That was both its essential strength and its weakness. By retaining a structure composed of communes, Defferre ensured that his legislation would be broadly acceptable, but left the problem of fragmentation to be tackled at some later stage. The Loi de l'Administration Territoriale de la République of 1992 was long in gestation but produced a solution that was close to that of the Guichard Report 16 years before. *Communautés de villes* and *communautés de communes* were to be created for urban and rural areas respectively across the country to ensure that a uniform system of intercommunal co-operation could come into existence. These groupings were not to be imposed upon communes, but prefects were required to draw up proposals for groupings in each of the *départements*. The legislation thus represents an extension of the classic principle of the syndical grouping. In *communautés de villes* the community would receive the whole of the employment tax of each of its constituent communes. Both types of community would be responsible for the *aménagement de l'espace* (spatial development) although whether that necessarily meant preparation of *POS* and control of development is not clear. At the time of writing it is not really possible to evaluate the effect of the legislation. There were only three *communautés de villes* by the beginning of 1993, but 193 *communautés de communes* and 82 new districts had been brought into existence (Delrue 1993). A year later the number of *communautés de communes* had risen to 517, but 40 more districts had been created. On the other hand, there were still only four *communautés de villes* (Dequéant 1994, Rivais 1994). There seems to be a clear preference for structures in which communes do not lose their power to set the level of local taxation.

The problem of uncertainty

However, another issue was beginning to dominate the debate on planning in the 1980s at the very moment when the success of the plan-making and control systems seemed to have been assured by decentralization. The Loi d'Orientation Foncière of 1967 had, as one of its objectives

> to battle against the uncertainty of the law and its correlative opacity . . . the wish was to require the administration – and local administrations above all – to replace the haggling over contingent decisions with rules of the game that are stable and transparent. (Auby 1987: 233–4)

At the very moment when a codified planning law with a structure of national and local regulations was being widely applied, the clarity and the stability that it was supposed to bring seemed to be under threat.

The sources of instability and opacity in the operation of planning law are various. The oldest of the problems that appeared to threaten the viability of the law was the problem of *dérogations* (departures) from the plan in force. The Loi d'Orientation Foncière of 1967 contained, as had its predecessors, the possibility of departing from an approved POS in order to respond to legitimate change in planning policy. Justifiable though the possibility was seen as being, the question of how far to allow departures has clearly been an agonizing one for the French, and has led to abuses (see Prats et al. 1979). After 1983 the law was changed so that all departures "save minor adaptations made necessary by the nature of the ground, the configuration of the site or the character of adjoining buildings" (Code de l'urbanisme, article L123–1). Inevitably, a complete interdiction on departures proved impossible to sustain and in 1986 the law was changed again to allow the application of rules in anticipation of the modification of a plan. The dilemma was nicely expressed by Danna & Driard (1991: 21):

> The imperious needs which drive decision-makers to adopt flexible means for modifying plans would soon lead to a return under form or another of the abhorred methods. Once again the phoenix would rise from its ashes.

For them the answer was to try to incorporate this kind of realism in an accountable fashion into the legislation, rather than to pretend it did not exist.

More recently the question of modifications and revisions to plans in force has been the subject of concern. The position has been most clearly expressed by Hocreitère (1991). Citing a report of the Conseil d'État of 1973 that had argued for "a minimum of stability without which there is no legal certainty". Hocreitère notes that the situation has hardly changed:

65

. . . the state of planning law seems to . . . have deteriorated to the point at which we can no longer talk of excessive movement but rather of a certain volatility. It is clear that the permanent process of evolution of planning regulations, and the way in which they are super- and juxtaposed, results in uncertainties, delays and insecurity. (93–4)

The problem is seen as all the greater because of the enormous increase in *POS* during the 1980s. The issue is clear: if plans are constantly in the process of modification, the expression of rights and duties that they contain is eroded, and development control decisions are at the mercy of administrative or political caprice.

A final cause of concern has been the ever-increased elaboration of planning law, both in the *Code de l'urbanisme* itself and in the regulations of *POS*. Two rather different strands of thought can be detected in this debate. One is that elaboration detracts from the purity of the law and leads to compromise and conflict:

. . . rules should be stable, clear, if possible precise, at all events objective, not lending themselves to argument; the judge's role being then a residual one, downstream, the ultimate longstop. (Bouyssou 1987: 321–2)

More recently the Conseil d'État, concerned with the rise in litigation in planning, has taken up the same theme. Among other things they noted the way in which attempts simplifying the *Code de l'urbanisme* had tended in practice simply to add to its complexity. *POS* are seen as documents that have increasingly strayed from the original intentions of planning law. The solutions included limitations on the content and the revision of *POS* and the elimination of *SD*, which were seen as posing irreconcilable problems for the determination of *permis de construire* because of slippage between *SD* and *POS*. The other strand of thinking is represented by Martin & Novarina (1987). They also see a danger in over-complexity in planning law, in that it gives decision-makers, be they elected representatives or officers of the state, the ability to develop their power base. Their recipe for reform is not so much to return the law to a primal simplicity as to give it greater flexibility. In that, they join another strand of official thinking that sees the current system of land-use plans as too inflexible to meet the demands of urban policy-making (Commissariat Général du Plan 1993).

Just as, with the British planning system, a discussion of the discretion to take planning decisions began to take us into deep waters, so too does this discussion of certainty and the rule of law in the context of France. What becomes clear is that the practice of development control in France is rooted in a conception of the nature of government and the role of law that is radically different from that in Britain. Once again the interest for present purposes is in the interaction between an understanding of the constitution and the objectives of controlling development.

CHAPTER 4

Zoning control in Europe, the USA and Hong Kong

So far, we have looked at the systems of controlling development in Britain and France as the unique product of the particular cultures of each country. In particular, we noted the traditions of law and administration had a direct bearing on the way in which development control systems had emerged and indeed on the central preoccupations of decision-makers. But Britain and France do not exist in isolation, and, as members of the European Union, they have increasingly been forced to consider systems of planning in other member-states. From the mid-1980s there has been a debate about what could be learned from other parts of Europe and whether there was scope for a unified planning system. In Britain, the publication of a major report on planning control in five member countries of the European Union in 1989 was a stimulus to this debate (Davies et al. 1989). Groups such as the Association of the European Schools of Planning (AESOP) and the European Town Planning Association have been instrumental in ensuring that common interests in both policy and process continue to be explored. There is an important case, therefore, for placing the British and French systems of control in the context of Europe.

However, there is a wider context that merits exploration. Any urbanized country sooner or later has to confront the problem of competing interests in land use, and institute a system of control that will resolve the conflict. They do so in ways dictated very largely by their culture of decision-making. But the adaptations their specific circumstances force them to make also illustrate more fundamental problems of the control process. In particular, they shed light on the themes that are the subject of this book. Two other systems are therefore used as points of reference. The first is that of the USA, sometimes, as the home of free enterprise, naïvely supposed to be opposed to any form of regulatory control, and as frequently seen as having the most highly developed system of zoning. The second, as different in scale as could be imagined, is that of Hong Kong, which has an administration that controls development, both as planning authority and landowner. The intention in this chapter is not to present a detailed account of the evolution of other systems of control, but to deal with particular issues to which these systems give rise.

Development control in Europe

Apart from the UK, Ireland has the only other planning system in Europe that lays comparable emphasis on flexibility and political discretion in decision-making, and only Ireland has succeeded, like Britain, in nationalizing the right to develop land (for a recent account of the Irish planning system, see Grist 1995). France, on the other hand has a system of control that draws many of its characteristics from an understanding of the purpose of law that is shared in mainland Europe. The first chapter made the distinction between the two families of development control represented by Britain and France respectively. Discretionary systems, characterized above all by the British planning system, institutionalize discretionary freedom in order to achieve flexibility. Regulatory systems are characteristic of mainland Europe. In all these systems there is an emphasis on legal certainty, and a codification of control powers. The specific circumstances of France may have led it in the end to adopt a regulatory system of control, but the choice also relates to an understanding of the nature of the state that is shared.

State, law and policy in Europe

The distinction between discretionary and regulatory systems of planning does not merely raise questions about the role of law. The nature of a country's legal system is itself a reflection of the concept of state, and the state's role in regulating the activities of its citizens. Deeply engrained in much of continental thinking is the concept of the *rechtsstaat* or *état de droit*: the state as created and defined by law. Indeed, the very concept of state divides Britain from continental Europe, for whereas in Germany and France the state is central to the discourse on government, the word has by and large been shunned in Britain (Dyson 1980). In continental Europe "the state was seen as a new element in society: a structure of authority and a mechanical organization of constraint" (ibid.: 34). It had, moreover, "a peculiar form of collective life whose nature and purpose needed to be identified" (ibid.: 35). Although these were ideas that led to constant debate, the important point is that they concentrated attention upon the concept of state itself, and upon the proper role of state within the nation. At least in part this was generated by a pragmatic response to powerful external threats to internal security. On the other hand, without that stimulus, Britain retained an essentially medieval pattern of government, and the increasing centrality of parliament with, from an early stage, territorial representation ensured that it became "the principal location for the articulation and aggregation of territorial interests" (ibid.: 39). To that then must be added the continuity of a medieval pattern of law, with its emphasis on judge-made law and its distance from politics. This was not a pattern that could serve to define the state. The state, such as it is in Britain, remains a collection of component parts, not a separate and definable entity, apart from civil society. That, coupled with the greater autonomy of local authorities, as Heidenheimer (1986) observes "kept cities from becoming the subject of a distinct body of law, legislation or administrative science" (ibid.: 12).

Within the general idea of state, however, continental Europe offers two theories that are to some extent in conflict with each other. Heidenheimer notes the difficulty faced in translating the term policy into French or German because of the overlap that exists with politics. On the other hand, the term "policey" [*sic*] was developed from the sixteenth century onwards in Germany "to designate legislative and administrative regulation of the internal civil life to promote general welfare" (ibid.: 12). From this then emerges the concept of the *polizeistaat*, which is in particular associated with the emergence of modern government in Brandenburg Prussia. It was a concept that had two distinct attributes, however. One side of the *polizeistaat* was the concern that it represented for the welfare of citizens. This concern ensured the state as an agency, separate from party or political idea, had a responsibility for social wellbeing. The other attribute of the *polizeistaat* was its capacity to be used in a totalitarian and oppressive manner. Dyson emphasizes the special status within society that the concept of the *polizeistaat* accords to the administrator. The administration and its officers become essential to ensuring the coherence of society. Continental European administrators thus carry a degree of responsibility denied to their British counterparts.

The theory of the *rechtsstaat* was all about the creation of the state as a legal construct. Dyson explained how this emphasis upon the legal state grew out of the dominance of legal scholars in unifying the legal systems of France and Germany and applying the principles of Roman law. Roman law provided both a unity and coherence for the system as a whole and a "body of concepts that were based on elaborate technical distinctions and would enable lawyers and judges to act with promptness and precision" (ibid.: 111). It demonstrates the preference for rationality and codification, and for rules over the judge-made laws of the British tradition. Above all, it ensured that the state distinguished between public and private affairs, which in turn paved the way for a separate body of administrative law and a separate system of administrative courts, of the kind we have already noted in France. The theory and practice of the *rechtsstaat* can thus be a means of restraining the totalitarian of repressive aspects of the *polizeistaat*. The whole concept of the codification of law in France, for all that it was introduced by a totalitarian regime, was nevertheless seen as a means of restraining the arbitrary and irrational exercise of royal power that had preceded the Revolution.

The point here is that this emphasis on the role of the state as a provider of welfare, on the role of the administration to guarantee the unity of the state, and the role of the law to provide rules to assist decision-making and to provide the means of redress for citizens, is not confined to France alone. Certainly, other countries of Europe have their particularities, but to a large extent have in common this understanding of law and state. Moreover, although the control of development in its modern form is a relative newcomer to the activities of government, this tradition of state and law has nevertheless had a critical bearing on the way control is perceived and put into effect. The first impact of this tradition on in the control of development, which we have already observed in France, is to systematize what in British terms would be referred to as policy as a system of legal rules. Within such a tradition, the plan becomes a localized expression of those rules. All decisions based upon these rules may be open to challenge, although often the conditions under which such challenge may be initiated are themselves prescribed by rules. Certainty is elevated into the major virtue of the system. The rights of individuals in relation to both land and development are underpinned.

Germany

There is an important case for considering Germany in this context. On the one hand, the concept of *rechtsstaat* and *polizeistaat* derive directly from German administrative science. On the other, the first thorough-going application of development control through zoning is to be found in Germany. England had studied German practice immediately before and after the passing of the 1909 Housing and Town Planning etc. Act; so too, both France and the USA looked to the German model in the period from the end of the nineteenth century. As with Britain and France, the earliest form of control was through a series of building regulations that appear to have been instituted in the Middle Ages. Logan (1976) notes that Munich had codified its ordinances by the end of the sixteenth century and, with additions, the code formed the basis of control until the nineteenth century. State governments became involved by the sixteenth century; and, by later in the nineteenth century, building regulations had become standardized across urban areas and detailed in their scope. Logan identifies 13 factors that were typically included in these regulations, varying from building lines applied both at both front and rear to architectural treatment, control over noxious uses and constructional detail:

> There was a trend towards more comprehensive coverage and a greater uniformity of application to the city area during the nineteenth century, replacing the earlier reliance on precedence and made-to-order negotiations for each new development. (Logan 1976: 379)

Regulations of this kind are an obvious example of the *polizeistaat* in operation.

The other impact of German planning that excited interest abroad was the power to create town extension plans where, once again, Germany was in advance of the rest of Europe. Powers to extend towns were in place from the early nineteenth century onwards and were linked to the increasing importance of municipal rather than state government, particularly in Prussia. Early town extension schemes showed road layouts that derived essentially from a modified Haussmannien model, coupled to the kind of building regulations described above (Sutcliffe 1981).

Why Germany should have taken the lead in this way requires explanation, the more so, as Sutcliffe remarks, because, judged by the outcomes, the quality of urban development in Germany was not higher than in other European countries in the nineteenth century. Part of the explanation has to do with the rapid industrialization of the country, which started much later than in Britain, although Germany had overtaken Britain by the 1880s. Part of the explanation has to do with the longstanding constriction of urban development imposed by fortifications and the urgent need for new development to prevent the evils of overcrowding. Part has to do with the fragmentation of landownership and the preference for investing in industry rather than in housing, which meant there was no development of a housebuilding industry, as occurred in England (Sutcliffe 1981). On the other hand, the involvement in planning has to do with an understanding of the state as regulator of human activities and as codifier of the rules by which both government and the population at large would abide, in order that the exercise of power was not arbitrary and that justice could be seen to be done. More decisively than other parts of Europe, Germany had emerged from the medieval world and had developed the liberal outlook of the enlightenment, which espoused freedom for the individual, rationality and central authority (van Gunsteren 1976). Building regulations ensured the liberty of the individual by requiring that others respected the individual's rights. Extension plans were intended to be rational and orderly, and to maintain the police power of the state.

The emergence of zoning in its modern form as a means of securing the control of development, comes with the passing of the Lex Adickes for Frankfurt-am-Main in 1891. What was achieved at Frankfurt was in effect a marriage of the regulations applied to buildings, with a concept of spatial planning contained in the town extension plans. The first stage of rationalizing planning was to standardize regulations across urban and suburban areas, rather than to continue *ad hoc* regulations for new development when it arose. The second stage was to realize that distinguishing between parts of the city was entirely appropriate if it was done consistently. The originals of the Lex Adickes at Frankfurt, which identified six distinct land-use zones to which different regulations would apply, came from a work by Baumeister, which had united the concerns of street layout plans with "a perceptive analysis of the trend towards greater separation of economically distinct land uses" (Logan 1976: 379). Logan makes the further point that the acceptance of zoning in Germany was closely linked to a perception that high land prices were caused by high densities that could be controlled through zoning ordinances. Finally, in German practice "the separation of land-uses was not a central objective" (ibid.: 383) because there was no desire to create exclusive zones, even though zoning did on occasions serve to protect the well to do.

Thus, the story that we have traced of the development of the French system of planning control, with its zoning and regulations deriving from a particular experience of urban growth and government, can usefully be seen in the wider context of an understanding of the nature and purpose of government. The early experience of Germany was formative, because the solution of coupling town extension schemes to regulations satisfied many of the preoccupations with the problem of controlling urban development. The system was scientific and rational. It breathed order into what could all too easily be chaotic. It provided clear rules for action by government and developers. It was not arbitrary and it served to protect rights and freedoms. Inevitably, what Germany started was picked up elsewhere and transformed, by the particular emphasis that reformers in different countries chose to place on the form of control and by the nature of the systems into which this particular control was grafted.

The Netherlands

The Netherlands also serve as a good example of the application of the *rechtsstaat* principle to planning and a useful point of comparison not only with France and England, but also with Germany. Van Gunsteren (1976) notes that the Dutch approach to administrative law is based heavily on German legal doctrine and that France is rather different. But the emphasis placed upon certainty and certainty under the law, which in turn has important ramifications for planning, recalls the same insistence that we remarked in relation to French planning. As van Gunsteren remarks, "The concept of legal certainty provides a key for the comparative analysis of legal systems" (ibid.: 80) and the same might be said of planning systems.

Certainly, the striking feature of the Dutch system of planning is the extent of control that is exercised. Indeed, the starting point for a description of the characteristics of the Dutch system has to be the system of plans. The basic planning document is the *bestemmingsplan*, introduced in 1962, but replacing an earlier system of *uitbreidingsplannen*, or town extension plans, dating from 1901, which applied only to suburban development on greenfield sites. Plans have to be prepared for all land outside the built-up area and may be applied to built-up areas where development is likely. Because plans produced under legislation do not lose their force, "virtually the entire surface area" (Davies 1988: 212) of the country is covered by legally binding plans. What has been an implied intention in French practice has, it appears, been put into effect in the Netherlands. Davies describes the *bestemmingsplan* thus: "The concept underlying the *bestemmingsplan* is that it identifies the 'destination' that is the form and use of every existing and proposed building or piece of land within the area of the plan. The purpose of control, then, is to ensure eventual "realization" of the plan. An application for a building permit must look first to the *bestemmingsplan* and then to the building regulations, over which the plan takes precedence (Davies 1988: 211).

The form of control exercised is, therefore, unlike France, through a plan and through regulations that have a separate existence. The regulations are indeed made under different legislation, and the law requires that every local authority has a set of such regulations. In part, these regulations are concerned with matters of building construction, safety and health. They also cover matters that would be material considerations in a British sense, or be part of the *POS* in France. The siting, specific location, relationships to surroundings of buildings are all included, as may be carparking, advertising and even demolition. They also deal with the general conditions under which change of use may occur, and with aesthetic control. They are, as Davies (1988: 211) puts it, "the only universal, legally binding source of policy and criteria for control covering the entire country . . .".

Two general principles appear to emerge from this description. The first is the desire to protect the liberty of the individual, paradoxically given the tight constraints that appear to be imposed through the *bestemmingsplan* and the building regulations. The important thing to note here is liberty is not expressed in terms of absolute rights to property. Unlike the case of France, property rights are not protected by the constitution, but by the civil code. There is none of the potential tension between property rights and regulatory control that exists in France, because property rights are subordinate to control by the legislation. Indeed, extensive public ownership of land is a feature of the country as an acknowledged means of defence against the sea and as a mechanism for promoting development.

The second principle arises from the first. The liberty that the law is designed to respect is achieved through the guarantee of certainty that the law accords. As Davies observes, there is no need for a general definition of development in the Dutch system of planning law, because the criteria for control are always specific to the local *bestemmingsplan* and to local regulations. The emphasis, then, in the Netherlands, appears to be on particularity, rather than on generality and on achieving control at the local level through a degree of democratic supervision of decisions. The French concern for unity and universality appears to be absent.

Something must also be said about the scope for modifying and departing from plans and regulations. The legislation that introduced the *bestemmingsplanen* in 1962 allowed very few possibilities for change or departure, although plans and regulations offered the possibility of defining limited freedom in relation to some criteria, such as specific categories of land use or building height. There were nevertheless specific possibilities for introducing flexibility, even under the 1962 legislation. The first, under Section 11 of the Act, concerned the possibility of describing planning policy for development or redevelopment in general terms to be elaborated in more detail at the point at which the development is about to proceed. The second, under section 19, is a procedure to permit development that goes beyond the parameters of the plan. Essentially, this procedure allows a municipality to issue a decree to the effect that the *bestemmingsplan* is to be revised or prepared, and this gives the right to the municipality to exercise interim control. Although this decree requires approval of both municipal and provincial authorities, and is based in part upon the results of public consultation, the procedure can nevertheless be swift. Since 1985, the ways of increasing the flexibility of plans have been increased. More variations from the plan for development are possible. Municipalities may describe in general terms the uses and their quantities in a given area, but are not obliged necessarily to specify precise locations.

In spite of these newer freedoms, the overwhelming impression of the Dutch system, as with the French, is one in which certainty is paramount. Nevertheless, the certainty has rather different origins and intentions. The strength of the tradition of local democratic decision-making is clearly significant in the way that it is not in France. So, too, there appears to be no search for general definitions and policy that will embrace the state as a whole and ensure its unity, as there is in France. The concept of the *rechtsstaat* and its application to planning has come from a rather different understanding of the relationship between the individual and the administration. But the mechanisms that are used to express those relationships are of the same kind.

The USA and zoning ordinances

Any discussion of planning control through zoning regulations, or of the interaction between systems of planning and constitutional rights, must include reference to the USA. Indeed, there are many features of the USA that make it relevant to the present discussion: its reputation as a culture of free enterprise in apparent contradiction to the tight regulations that zoning control imposes in many urban areas; the large role that constitutionality has played in decision-making in planning; the refinements that have been brought to the practice of zoning by ambitious city authorities. However, the USA does present a significant problem in its scale and diversity. In Europe we may talk of the unified practice of control and the consistency of general principles and their application in the member-states of the European Union. In the USA, by contrast, practice is enormously varied. Neither planning instruments nor mechanisms of control, nor yet again systems of administration and decision-making, are constant across the country. There is not even consistency within individual states: state powers in planning are weak, and control, together with the zoning and regulations that form the basis for control, is in the hands of a multiplicity of development control authorities, albeit within the limits of the powers conferred on them by state legislation. There are, within the USA as a whole, some 50 different systems of local government (Cullingworth 1993). Nevertheless, out of this welter of particularities, several general issues emerge that shed light on the themes we are exploring in relation to Britain and France.

The origins and purpose of US zoning control

The earliest forms of control exercised in US urban areas were evidently similar to the kinds of building regulations that were used in London. Moreover, until independence, it was generally accepted that eminent domain – the right of government to acquire land compulsorily – "was an inherent power of government for which specific regulation was not required" (Cullingworth 1993: 21). However, the adoption of the Constitution and the Bill of Rights had a profound impact. On the one hand, as Cullingworth notes, limiting the power of government to acquire land arbitrarily without new compensation became a key issue for the courts. On the other, the supreme court acquired the "singular power to determine the constitutionality of legislative action" (ibid.: 22). This is significant because it is the application of the law that is subject to the challenge on the grounds of constitutionality, unlike France where the Conseil Constitutionnel and the Conseil d'État consider the laws and regulations before they are finally enacted (Brown & Bell 1993). It is significant, too, in that the question of land-use and development rights and their control became an issue bound up in the general understanding of citizenship and the nature of the state.

Although constitutionality and the rights of individuals are central to the nature of development control in the USA, the emphasis upon rights and the abhorrence of unconstitutional action did not mean that America shunned planning. At very much the same time as Europe was moving towards comprehensive planning, so, too, in the USA there was an upsurge of interest in the idea of controlling urban areas for reasons of both sanitation and aesthetics. To some extent, there was already a precedent in the USA for the controls that would be introduced by zoning ordinances. The police powers and regulations that existed in US cities with the aim of ensuring the health and moral welfare of their residents were already recognized as having a sound constitutional basis, and early planning reformers argued that land-use planning control would be no more than an extension of these police powers. There is a clear link here to the European *polizeistaat* concept. But the inspiration for the use of the zoning control mechanism came from elsewhere.

Just as in France and England, the early protagonists of planning cast envious eyes towards Germany, so too did the pioneers in the USA. The particular focus for the interest was the Chicago World Fair in 1893 and the City Beautiful movement to which it gave rise. If the City Beautiful movement did not itself directly produce action, it did appear to raise the level of general awareness, and it led to the creation of permanent city planning commissions (Scott 1969). The impetus towards detailed control and the application of the German technique of zoning, came not from the desire to beautify the city but the will to understand its nature through the application of scientific principles. Thus, F. L. Olmsted Jnr "hoped to master the complexities of the visible city 'through better knowledge of facts, clearer definition of purpose, and through improvements of technique'" (Scott 1969: 123). Various authorities began to advocate municipal action to control land use, by separating out factory districts and controlling building density in residential districts. Zoning came to be seen as "a heaven-sent nostrum for sick cities" (Scott 1968: 192; cited by Cullingworth 1993: 21):

Once the idea of protecting both residential and industrial areas from incompatible activities presented itself, the adaptation of German zoning to US purposes seemed all the more desirable. City planning then became a matter of altering spatial relationships to achieve the practical ends of efficiency and convenience. (Scott 1969: 123)

Popular support for zoning control began to increase and zoning came to assume a prominence in the debate on planning, to the despair of those who advocated the preparation of plans before zoning was introduced. The first tentative steps to introduce zoning control date from the beginning of the century: in Los Angeles in 1909, then in Wisconsin, Minnesota and Illinois and finally, and most influentially, in New York City in 1916. Although theorists might argue that zoning needed to depend on a rigorously scientific approach contained in a city-wide plan, the New York ordinance was conspicuously not based on such a plan.

The final stage in the acceptance of zoning control came with the inevitable test of its constitutionality from the years after the New York ordinance had been passed. The case of the *Village of Euclid* vs *Ambler Realty* in 1926 is always cited as the watershed in the legal history of planning and as a famous victory for zoning. The essential question that Ambler Realty wished to test was whether the zoning ordinance for the village of Euclid (a suburb of Cleveland, Ohio) was

invalid in that it violates constitutional protection to the right of property in the appellee by attempted regulations under the guise of police power, which are unreasonable and confiscatory. (Rose 1969: 78)

Rose goes further to define the general constitutional question that zoning gives rise to as threefold: that zoning must be within the general scope of police power to protect the "health, safety, morality and welfare of the community"; that zoning must not be so harsh as to violate the principal of the due process of law; and that zoning must be non-discriminatory (ibid.: 75). The "victory" of Euclid was to show that zoning need not be unconstitutional, and the judgement paved the way for the Standard Zoning Enabling Act, which became the foundation of modern US zoning. More than that, as Haar & Kayden (1989) remark, "It is easy to forget how completely zoning and its near universal adoption have recast the terms for the debate. Today's arguments are about how far, not whether, private property must yield to the public weal" (ibid.: ix).

The importance of zoning in the US system and the emphasis on zoning in preference to plan preparation, particularly in the face of the constitutional right to property, require more explanation than can be offered by case law from the Mid-West. Indeed, the literature suggests two important reasons why zoning should have achieved such widespread acceptance after the Euclid case, which have nothing to do with constitutionality. Boyer (1980: 153) argues:

Zoning, the division of the US city into a structure of cells, hierarchically controlled and re-arranged, was a technical solution meant to secure an orderly and stable development of the urban land market. Promoting a disciplinary order, with its values of efficiency and functionality, already etched out in the planning mentality by 1914, the core purpose of zoning was to remove and separate conflicting land-uses and dysfunctional districts that might impede or destroy solid investments in land. Never meant to tamper with the ethic of private property, US zoning was intended instead to secure the interest of property owners by enhancing the economic stability of home ownership and promoting the speculative development of real estate in the center of American cities.

On the one hand, then, zoning was about protecting residential property values in both a financial and a moral sense. Zoning was a way of protecting single-family residential areas from the unwelcome incursion of either industrial and commercial uses or apartment houses. In this, zoning would be attractive to residents of such areas, and to the politicians responsible for introducing the ordinances. As Rabin (1989: 134) puts it: "The basic purpose of zoning . . . was to maintain the American dream". On the other hand, zoning was positively welcomed by real-estate developers because of the order that it breathed into the markets in land for development (Haar 1989). Thus, the early ordinances for Los Angeles were very largely the result of pressure from developers "who shrewdly identified land-use regulation . . . as an important vehicle for strengthening Los Angeles' most appealing selling point." (Rabin 1989: 103). So, too, the introduction of zoning-enabling legislation in Wisconsin, Minnesota and Illinois was the result of pressure from home-owners and real-estate developers alike (Scott 1969). Behind this acceptance lies the economic growth of the 1920s, within which zoning could be seen as "a disciplinary movement designed to facilitate the development of domestic consumption patterns and to stabilize center city property values" (Boyer 1980: 168). A symbiosis had been created between the real-estate market, the aspirations of US home-owners and the desire for regulatory control through zoning.

Zoning or planning: the US dilemma

The intentions of the advocates of zoning as a scientific means for enhancing order, safety and health in cities in modern America had always been that zoning would be the mechanism by which policy in a strategic planning document would be implemented. In particular, the Standard Zoning Enabling Act required zoning regulations to "be made in accordance with a comprehensive plan" (cited by Cullingworth 1993: 12). However, we have already noted how the New York ordinance of 1916, which was to set the pattern for the rest of the country, was made in the absence of a plan. But the problem was not just the absence of a plan, it was also a question of the preoccupations of the plan-makers. Scott notes that the "overriding consideration" of the planning team was to ensure that the ordinance was constitutional and could "meet the narrowest and most legalist interpretation of the phrases 'public welfare' and public health, safety, morals and convenience". The New York ordinance met the challenge of legality but resulted in a document that was "extremely conservative" and whose "provisions lacked the broader justification of far-sighted planning to meet new and unforeseen conditions" (ibid.: 155). Thus, the underlying concern with constitutionality, which did not disappear with the Euclid case, came to influence the manner in which zoning ordinances were prepared, and accentuated the division between zoning and planning.

This division remains a reality to the present day, such that zoning ordinances are to be found in almost every urban area in the USA, but plans are not. Unlike the French *POS*, zoning ordinances were never intended to be a policy document. They nevertheless have come to be the sole means by which land-use policy at the local level is defined. Interestingly, however, this concept of an implementation device for policies in a plan, which seems from a European perspective to be unassailable, does not find favour in all quarters of US thinking. Thus, while Babcock (1966) argues that zoning is indeed about planning and the "disclosure of municipal objectives [in a plan] may be a necessary first step by which equal treatment of similarly situated individuals within a municipality can be determined", he is vigorous in his opposition to the municipal land-use plan as the sole measure of consistency for local zoning regulations (ibid.: 122). Moreover, the way in which zoning ordinances are used is an indication of how different as a mechanism they are from European zoning plans. Cullingworth, for example, observes that

> A European observer would expect that zoning had a great deal to do with the management of development on the urban fringe . . ., but he would be sadly wrong . . . The cumulative effect of lot decisions tends to be ignored and municipalities, largely in favour of development, have tended to be unconcerned with timing. (ibid: 123)

What begins to emerge from this discussion is that zoning in the USA is a good deal more complex than it would at first appear. A system derived from Europe, where it had been geared to the orderly extension of towns and the management of existing urban areas, had become little by little transmuted into an instrument seen as compatible with the Constitution – and, by extension, something that confirmed constitutional rights – and useful for protecting the individual homeowner and regulating the activities of the development industry. At the same time it has clearly served the ends of pro-development municipalities. The one thing it appears not to have been about is planning in the European sense. Its characteristics and the way in which it is used shed interesting light on the question of controlling development. We need, therefore, to turn to the current practice of zoning in the USA.

Making changes: The possibilities for modifying zoning ordinances

Wakeford (1990: 3), in his study of US development control from a British perspective, argues that the British and US systems were moving in opposite directions. Where the British system was aiming for greater certainty in development control decision-making, "the movement in the USA seems to be in the opposite direction – towards less certainty for the developer. What the zoning ordinance permits seems less and less likely to be what the developer himself would want to pursue". If the antithesis seems facile, and it is substantially qualified later on in Wakeford's work, there is nevertheless an important perception of the system that has found a multitude of ways in which to apply ordinances. Cullingworth stresses that "Zoning is an inherently rigid instrument . . . and in this rigidity lies its enormous popular appeal. The planning ideal of flexibility is anathema to protectionist home-owners. Rigidity gives them certainty and security. This he notes "remains so in spite of the extraordinary ingenuity . . . which has been displayed in adapting [zoning] to the real moving world" (ibid.: 33). These adaptive mechanisms are worth exploring because of the light they shed upon the wider problems of development control decision-making. The classic way of overcoming the rigidity of the zoning system was through the issuing of variances. The intention had originally been that seeking a variance would be an exceptional action, but has developed to become very much the standard practice, as the quotation from Wakeford implies. Variances are essentially the way in which intending developers seek to overcome the rigidity of zoning. For the municipality, however, there is a different need. Rose (1969: 147) suggests that there are four preconditions for zoning on the Euclid model to be effective:

1. That planners can predict the nature and quantities of community's *needs* with some precision and exactitude;
2. That planners can, with accuracy, convert the quantification of community needs into an allocation and designation of land-use;
3. That the economic and political forces within the community will respond compliantly with these designations;
4. That the very act of designation as specified zones for prescribed uses will not undermine the achievement of this community's goals and objective.

Although Rose presents zoning as part of a rational planning process, and not at heart concerned primarily with residential protection, the quotation does reveal the inherent problem with zoning: that however well it may address home-owners' needs for security, it cannot always respond to developers' and municipalities' desires to promote development.

Where therefore Rose's preconditions are not met, or developers' needs cannot be accurately predicted, a series of devices have been created that attempt to address this unpredictability in the planning process. These divide into three kinds: those that do not tightly define regulations for a given area in order to

79

allow continued mix of land uses of use or negotiation with a developer in the event of development proceeding; those that fix regulations for a given use but without specifying the location; and those that allow landowners, developers and municipalities to trade development rights in accordance with the regulations against some kind of community benefit. The ingenuity of all these devices is not in question, but it is also clear that they cause considerable concern within the USA. Babcock (1966: 11) sees zoning as having slipped from "the simple, open-faced text to highly complex documents" and in so doing creating "total confusion". Cullingworth (1993: 59) states baldly:

> It is abundantly clear that zoning is not the rigid, simple system of land-use regulation that it is intended to be. In fact it is not rigid: it displays remarkable flexibility. It is not simple: it is increasingly complex.

US zoning, which appears to have achieved its acceptance by appealing to the needs of home-owners, developers and municipalities through a single mechanism, actually conceals some serious tensions. Some of these are to do with the respect for constitutionality and due process being inevitably in conflict with the desire to loosen the rigidity of zoning to meet particular circumstances. Some are to do with the desire of home-owners to seek certainty in the knowledge that undesirable uses are excluded from their (single-family) zone being in opposition to municipalities' genuine uncertainty about future needs and developers' desire to negotiate advantage beyond the limits imposed by an ordinance.

The final point that must be made about zoning has to do with the nature of the administration for planning. Zoning is, we have already noted, a creature of the municipalities, and something in which neither state nor federal government have a role, except through the provision of enabling legislation. The problem here seems to be twofold. The first is that municipalities are often very small and the kind of public interest they serve is narrowly focused (Cullingworth 1993). Babcock's distrust of the municipal plan as the justification for a zoning ordinance (in practice, as we have noted, a rare occurrence in any case) is because such a plan would itself be based upon a narrow self-interest:

> The trouble then with the Planning Theory of zoning is that by deifying the municipal plan it enshrines the municipality at a moment in our history when every social and economic consideration demands that past emphasis on the municipality as the repository of "a general welfare" be rejected" (Babcock 1966: 123).

In particular, Cullingworth notes that there is no mechanism for allocating "undesirable but socially necessary" uses. The other problem that Cullingworth identifies is in effect a constitutional issue. The US system of government is based upon a rigid separation of legislative and executive functions. This means at the local level that, although the municipality prepares the zoning ordinance, it is left to an independent zoning commission to deal with variances from zoning in force, and any appeal arising from the commission's decisions are taken by a

Board of Adjustment. This inevitably has the effect of attenuating the consistency with which the ordinance is applied and thereby undermining whatever rationale may lie behind its pattern of zones.

Cullingworth concludes that US zoning control is not just a rigid system, it is not a unified system at all in the sense that we can talk about British or French development control. It is rather a loose bundle of practices implemented in very different ways by disparate local authorities, which operate under a series of general concepts of constitutional freedoms, private property rights and police powers. Cullingworth also suggests that the idea that courts give a coherence to the system is false. Their major interest is in constitutionality and not in the appropriateness of the decision, and the judgments state courts reach are often inconsistent across the country. The essential interest in America for present purposes, therefore, is in the underlying tensions already described and not in the specifics of the system.

Hong Kong: government as landlord

Moving from the vastness and complexity of the USA to the tightly circumscribed territory of Hong Kong might seem simply absurd, the more so given the highly specialized nature of Hong Kong's administration. Neither its culture nor its conditions appear to invite any direct comparison with Europe or the USA. Nevertheless, Hong Kong raises a series of interesting questions about the relationship of landownership to systems of control in the public interest and the activities of the real-estate industry. Rather as with USA, there is an apparent paradox that the territory that in the 1980s became synonymous with the burgeoning spirit of free enterprise should in fact have a highly regulated system of land-use control. The interest in Hong Kong, however, is to do with the extent to which the government itself has a stake in the development process. There is, moreover, a second interest in that, although the basic land-use control is a form of zoning of a type unknown in Britain, the government nevertheless operates according to principles that are essentially British. The emphasis upon flexibility and discretionary decision-making that we saw as hallmarks of British administration for planning, deriving from a wider culture of law and government, are also present in Hong Kong. These must co-exist with a desire for certainty that is reflected in, and in part created by, a system of zoning.

The origins of land-use control in Hong Kong

The origins of Hong Kong's system of land-use control go back to the very moment that the island of Hong Kong was ceded to the British by the Treaty of Nanjing in 1842. A Land Office and a Land Committee were set up even before Hong

Kong was declared a colony in 1843 (Bristow 1984, Yeh 1994). As a Crown Colony it has no written constitution and:

> the whole of the government lies within the prerogative powers of the Crown
> . . . It is important to stress the importance of the royal prerogative . . .
> not only because it dictates the form of government, but also because those
> who reside within the colony, whether British subjects or not, have no constitutional right to interfere or make demands of the Crown in the exercise
> of the prerogative. (Evans 1971: 21)

In particular the Crown was to exercise from the outset far closer controls over the title to property than in Britain. The reasons for this are now purely historical and are to do with the distinction between real and personal property, abolished in Britain in the 1920s. Land, as "real" property was subject to "excessively complicated rules" but leases issued for a term of years were always considered to be personal property:

> There was, therefore, a positive advantage to be gained in terms of administrative simplicity if Hong Kong were to have no "real property" at all.
> (Evans 1971: 24)

It was thus arranged that all land should be held on leases granted by the Crown. In that way, the role of the Hong Kong government is, as Evans observes, comparable with that of the aristocratic landlords of eighteenth-century London.

In theory, this combination of ground landlord and government authority should have given Hong Kong government unparalleled power over the form of development and an effective means for ensuring the compliance with long-term planning policy. However, in the nineteenth century there was not, in Hong Kong, or elsewhere, an equivalent to a modern understanding of the planning process – which emerged in Europe and the USA only at the very end of the century – and very much as in London in the heyday of aristocratic development, there were only limited attempts to control the overall form of the development that was taking place. But development was by no means entirely sporadic, as Bristow observes. A programme of public works, particularly concerned with waterfront reclamation, represents one kind of attempt to impose overall control; the measures taken in the interests of public health, modelled on contemporary British practice, were another. For the rest, however, there was plenty of activity in laying out roads and plots for buildings:

> Where land form permitted, the land-leasing system produced the familiar
> rectangular gridiron street pattern of the nineteenth century colonial town,
> its dimensions determined by the minimum street layout regulations and
> the building requirements of the Chinese tenement houses, or European-
> type dwellings, depending on the area examined . . . Later problems arose
> because the plans were largely drawn up to meet immediate requirements.
> (Bristow 1984: 27)

The first major effort to plan for urban development in a co-ordinated way did not emerge until after the First World War, with the Town Planning Scheme of 1922, whose principal impact is visible in the grid-iron street pattern of the Kowloon peninsula. 九龍街形式 Although in many ways this represented a real effort at defining the nature and form of future development, and made allocations for public uses, the 1922 plan did not, unlike the contemporary planning schemes of Britain, have a statutory force, and it was given effect only by the process of issuing leases for buildings. The plan was essentially a modern version of the leasing plans of the previous two centuries, albeit on a very large scale. Interestingly, in spite of its having an advisory rather than a mandatory force, it appears to have fuelled the speculation in land to which it was intended as a response. Just as in the USA, the activities of the government (in this case as landlord) were beginning to set up a relationship of dependency with the users and developers of the land. Yet, at the same time, the actual level of control exercised over the use of land was minimal, apart from building envelope controls that dated from the 1903 Building Ordinance. Bristow (1984: 58) argued that:

> . . . the real failure of the years [before 1941] was not in the preliminary planning, but in the collapse of any effective collaboration between the government and property owners . . . It was through the efforts of the property owners rather than the strength of enforcement action, that Hong Kong became the city that it was.

Conditions in Hong Kong after the end of the Japanese occupation forced the administration to take a renewed interest in town planning. Indeed, a planning ordinance had already been approved in 1939, although the War had prevented any action, apart from the nomination of members of a Town Planning Board. In 1948 Abercrombie visited Hong Kong and proposed a development plan on the model of those to be prepared under the 1947 Town and Country Planning Act in Britain. But within the colony the move was towards developing zoning and density controls, which could be applied and enforced generally, rather than to a system of planning of the kind that was being introduced in Britain. Development rights were in effect already vested in the Crown in Hong Kong and needed no legislative action of the kind that has led to their nationalization in Britain. What was required was a system that gave some order to the process of issuing leases and minimized the adverse impact of the new development on neighbouring property. The result was the Building (Planning) Regulations of 1956, which specified a wide range of reasons for refusing building plans, with a new procedure for appeals against refusals. The regulations also made possible much higher plot ratios than had been permitted hitherto, resulting in the very high densities that are now characteristic of much of urban Hong Kong. Meanwhile, however, the 1939 Planning Ordinance was in effect revived: the reinstatement of the Town Planning Board in 1947 could have led to the development of new legislation, but by 1951, when the Board first met, pressure was for the preparation of Outline Development Plans and layouts for unbuilt areas, but not for the further creation of strategic plans. The emphasis was on preparing the way for immediately realizable development.

Gradually, the early Outline Development (later called Outline Zoning) Plans came to acquire a higher profile. The Building Ordinance of 1956 "made it mandatory for the building authority to refuse consent for building works which contravened approved plans and discretionary concerning draft plans prepared under the Planning Ordinance" (Bristow 1984: 78).

In the same year, draft plans had to be made available to the public on demand. Plans produced were from the beginning detailed zoning plans that specified the uses to be permitted and certain limited exceptions. The general regulations of the Building Ordinance governed the actual form of buildings that would then result.

This system has become increasingly sophisticated, but has not been fundamentally altered. There has been, since the development pressures of the 1970s, a renewed interest in strategic planning, such that there are now plans for the territory as a whole, for the five subregions, as well as Outline Zoning Plans and the administrative departmental plans at district level. Outline Zoning Plans themselves were modified in the Town Planning Ordinance of 1974. This formalized the concept of as-of-right ("Column 1") uses and those ("Column 2") uses for which the Town Planning Board was given a discretion to permit, although the practice goes back to the earliest of the Outline Zoning Plans to be made public, as is evident from North Point plan that Bristow (1984: 80–81) reproduces. What was new in the 1974 amendment was the introduction of a system of planning permissions for those "Column 2" uses separate from the lease covenant approvals of the Buildings Authority. A further change was made by the amendments of the Town Planning Ordinance of 1991, which introduced the concept of the Development Permission Area, specifically for rural areas in the New Territories, which by the 1980s were coming under considerable pressure for often harmful development. These Development Permission Areas introduced a degree of discretionary decision-making, so far absent in the Hong Kong planning system, in that although they could identify as-of-right uses, any other use required a planning permission. The 1991 Amendment did, moreover, introduce a system of enforcement against non-conforming uses in Development Permission Areas (Hong Kong 1991), but this is to be understood not as enforcement against failure to apply for planning permission, but against uses that did not conform to the uses permitted by the Development Permission Area. In parallel to the legislative changes, the administration for planning was also being developed from a small unit in the Public Works Department to a separate Planning Department under its own director, within the Planning Environment and Land Branch in 1990 (Yeh 1994).

The essential characteristics of the development control system are its reliance on zoning at the detailed planning level and the application of policies largely through the use of leasehold covenants. Onto this basic structure has then been grafted aspects of the British "permitting system" (the description of the US lawyer, Babcock, of British development control). This curious hybrid was the subject of a comprehensive review that was intended to lead to new legislation in 1995, but the amendments proposed by the review have yet to be laid before Legislative Council and may well not be enacted before Hong Kong reverts to Chinese control in 1997.

The Hong Kong system in perspective

The fact that the system of control in Hong Kong is a hybrid of zoning, discretionary control and leasehold control, and the fact that within the territory itself the system has given rise to prolonged heart-searching in the 1990s, raises some interesting questions. Why has the system been perceived to have been relatively ineffective in controlling development? The aristocratic landlords of the eighteenth century, to whom Evans likened the Crown in Hong Kong, after all achieved Draconian control over their property, and the accepted wisdom in Britain has been that those who have control over landownership are likely to have a greater degree of success in ensuring the right development in the right place at the right time. The answer appears both to do with the interests of the government and the nature of the mechanism.

The interests of the government are straightforward. Since the nineteenth century, sales of leases have always been a significant proportion of the government's revenue. Although the proportion has dropped sharply in the 1990s, sales have averaged more than 8 per cent of the revenue in the 16 years between 1974 and 1990 and in the peak year of 1981 exceeded 35 per cent (Yeh 1994). In addition to the specific interest in raising revenue, the government has also been anxious to ensure the continued prosperity of the territory, which from the 1980s has been increasingly associated with land development. The government, therefore, had a twofold desire to ensure that development took place: to ensure the long-term future of the territory and in the short term to maintain a useful source of income. The overriding desire on the part of government was not to restrain development, but to create the conditions under which development could take place to the best advantage. Of course that meant, among other things, that some uses had to be restricted in order to ensure that neighbouring developments were not adversely affected. The zoning plans and as-of-right uses created a degree of certainty for developers that also assisted the process of land valuation for the government. Leasehold control, therefore, seems to have involved finding a balance between minimizing constraints on development to maximize profits for government and developer, and imposing constraints to mitigate the adverse effects of competition to create profit.

The problem with the nature of the mechanism is more complex. Eighteenth-century landlords in London and elsewhere in the UK achieved a tight degree of control over development because their interests were no so much in short-term revenue as in long-term increase in capital value. The overriding desire was to improve the capital value of land and, more significantly, to maintain the improve-

85

ment to the end of the increasingly standard 99-year lease. This, landlords learned, was achieved by rigorous enforcement of construction standards, and sometimes also control over uses (Booth 1980). In this, the Hong Kong government's concern would appear almost from the outset to have been the reverse: a much greater emphasis on immediate returns from lease premiums than on capital value. This seems to have resulted in encouraging minimal controls on building form and uses, except in so far as there was exclusionary zoning to prevent the encroachment on "European" areas by Chinese development (Bristow 1984). However, there is a fundamental problem with leasehold control. The leasehold represents a contract between landlord and lessee that spells out what the lessee may or may not do with the land. The terms of the lease may be more or less stringent. Once signed, however, the lease confers rights on the lessee that endure for the life of the lease, and these not infrequently have proved problematic. Early leases granted with minimum constraints in Hong Kong have led to development that has embarrassed the government. So, too, more recently, changes of use in Kowloon have led to the rapid degradation of a residential area (Hong Kong 1991). The only way in which these problems can be resolved is through the resumption of the lease by the landlord, which is a costly process. It is important to be clear that these problems with leasehold control are not unique to Hong Kong. Cullingworth, in commenting upon Houston in the USA, which boasts that it is the one major city without a zoning ordinance, but nevertheless uses restrictive covenants to achieve some of the same ends, notes how ineffective leasehold covenants have proved to be.

Public controls over development were introduced in Britain because in the end, in spite of the refinements that had been brought to leasehold control, leases were not an adequate means of preventing slum building or overcrowding. This was particularly true where there was a short-term need to raise income from property, which outweighed the interest to protect capital values. Local authorities increasingly wanted to step in to make good the deficiencies in landlords: control could be undertaken according to objective criteria established to protect the public good by an agent outside the development process. Hong Kong has also long since realized the need for other controls other than those exercised by a landlord. Public health regulations could be built fairly easily into lease covenants, but in the post-war period the need for regulatory control through zoning to protect property values of adjacent plots has also come to be seen as an acceptable form of intervention. The process of reconciling the revenue-earning objectives with those of strategic planning has been far harder. Government, with a major stake in the success of the development process, finds it hard to assume the role of arbiter of the public good, or indeed to keep the revenue-earning and the strategic planning objectives separate.

Another kind of confusion of roles is also a problem. Not only is the government landlord and planning authority, it is the only source to whom objectors can turn for redress against decisions. Indeed, in a leasehold system there is very little right for the public at large to become involved in what is essentially a private process between landlord and lessee, as the 1974 system of planning applications excluded the public from the decision-making process altogether. When an applicant appeals against a development control decision, the government is effectively judge in its own case. An applicant appeals to the Town Planning Board, which was itself the final authority for the original decision. That will be to some extent mitigated by the introduction of a separate Appeal Board, but initial decision and appeal are still located in close proximity.

Conclusion

What the German, Dutch, US and Hong Kong systems thus illustrate is that it is not enough to look at procedures and control mechanisms to discover how a development control system works. The four cases demonstrate very clearly an interlocking pattern of theories of government and state, patterns of law and legal relationships, and the question of landownership and property rights. In all four cases, a particular mechanism, zoning, has served to relate those three factors and to minimize conflict between them, even if zoning is evidently not intended to achieve the same kind of ends in each of the four places. Nevertheless, within the differences, all four systems lay emphasis on rights and on certainties. The interesting point is that the rights and certainties in question are different. In the Netherlands and Germany the initial preoccupation is to deal with the right of government to govern, impartially, in the best interests of its citizens. This in turn has begged the question of "Government by what authority?" and has led to the *rechtsstaat* principle discussed above. This, among other things, has confirmed the individual's right to property and the certainty of redress in law if the government exceeds its authority. In the USA, the emphasis seems to be more heavily on guarantees to the rights of individuals, and in zoning for residents of an area to achieve the certainty of protection for their life-style. But as we saw in the USA, too, certainty for developers through the creation of an ordered land market was a key factor. Certainty for developers is repeatedly stressed in Hong Kong as a virtue of the Outline Zoning Plans. In Hong Kong, however, another kind of certainty is as important: certainty for the government in the management of its estate.

The certainties and rights that zoning may confer are clearly not intended to be of the same order. There is, moreover, a question as to whether these different zoning systems achieve what they were intended to do. Do they deliver the certainties upon which they appear to be premised, do rights and certainties ever conflict and, if so, how is the conflict resolved? And what do these systems do when faced with uncertainty and change? It is to these questions that we now need to turn.

CHAPTER 5
The question of certainty

In describing the French and British systems of development control, and in setting them in the context of practice in Europe, the USA and Hong Kong, the question of certainty has recurred constantly. In a sense this is perhaps hardly surprising, since planning by its very nature is about trying to predict future patterns of land use and development. Nevertheless, the ways in which the planning systems described deal with the question of certainty seem very different. France, we noted, appears to place a high premium upon certainty above all else, and the certainty in question is that of outcome, that anyone involved in the development process may know in advance what is, and what is not, permissible. Britain, on the other hand, appears to have no such concern and has instead sought to ensure that its system is flexible rather than certain. Yet even in Britain the question of certainty has never been far from the surface. Part of the debate, as in France, is about certainty of outcome; but lurking behind the debate on delay seems to be an issue of certainty of process, of knowing when you can expect a decision as well as what that decision will be. An initial question is, therefore, that of how the French and British systems of development control deal with certainty. To that, however, must be added others. What kind of certainty do in fact these two systems manage to deliver? And secondly, to what extent to the different actors in the development process require certainty in the control process?

Developers and certainty

During the 1980s orthodox political wisdom held that the free market was by and large the best judge of where and when development should take place. Bureaucratic control by local authorities should as far as possible be reduced. We noted in Chapter 2 that the British government's policy advice had stressed in the early 1980s the discretion that local authorities had to approve development when it was necessary to boost the supply of housing or the local economy, even in the face of planning policy contained within plans. Plans could be safely disregarded if they were "out of date" (DoE 1985); the existence of an identified five-year supply of housing land was not a reason for refusing housing development on other land (DoE 1984a); above all, Structure plans seemed to offer nothing at all to a proper process of development (Parliament 1989). The development control process would be about facilitating development, making sure that land was available when needed, defining the necessary level of services and infrastructure. The response of the House Builders' Federation to the government's White Paper suggested that this was far from being the whole truth. Humber (1989), then President of the Federation, argued that planners and developers had a common interest and that plans played an important part in the process of development. The tone is markedly more conciliatory than Baron's had been at the beginning of the decade, although as we noted, even Baron, while expressing his irritation with the planning system, was not wholly opposed to it. Developers only objected to control where it became needlessly involved in matters of trivial detail. The truth appears to be, that, just as with US zoning ordinances, the development industry in Britain needs planning control to reduce the risks inherent in a wholly free market. Some degree of certainty of outcome is important, and the planning system can help deliver it.

Certainty of outcome

Nevertheless, if certainty is perceived as important by the development industry, there is evidence to suggest that absolute certainty is not what is being looked for, particularly if that certainty is outright rejection. Consider the case of Foxley Wood in Hampshire referred to in Chapter 2. Emboldened by the apparent policy stance of the DOE's Circular on housing land, a group of developers had come together as Consortium Developments to promote housing in the South East on land that had hitherto been considered inviolable: in the green belt, or on "white land", that is land unallocated in development plans. The argument put forward by the developers was that the government was known to favour a market-led solution to the problems of housing in the South East, and that if development proposals were for complete new settlements, the developments might prove difficult to oppose at the local level. The consortium's proposal at Tillingham Hall, in the London green belt between Upminster and Basildon, was rejected on appeal; but here the issue rested entirely on the question of the purpose of the green belt to prevent the coalescence of urban areas, a definition that was still present in unequivocal terms in the current Circulars. Foxley Wood was a more likely candidate because it was to be located on white land in northeast Hampshire, a county that had already made adequate provision for housing in its approved structure plan. Here, the exhortation of Circular 15/84 (DOE 1984a) seemed appropriate: there was no prima facie case for refusing the development just because housing land allocations were made in other parts of the county. Moreover, the developers worked hard to allay local objections by, for example, offering protection to a Site of Special Scientific Interest that formed part of the area to be developed. There appears to have been some conflict within government itself as to the correct course of action. In a curious formulation, Nicholas

Ridley, Secretary of State for the Environment, declared that he was "minded to allow" the proposal, and this not-quite-a-decision was supported by a positive statement by the then junior minister responsible for planning, Michael Howard. The likelihood is that Nicholas Ridley was more sensitive to the political harm that such a decision would cause than was his junior minister. When, after a political indiscretion, Ridley was replaced as Secretary of State, his successor, Chris Patten, moved swiftly to reject the proposal (*Planner* 1989a, 1989b).

There are two ways in which this story can be interpreted. The ambiguities of central government policy suggested a distinctly relaxed attitude to what would have hitherto been unacceptable development. By virtue of the generalization of Circular 15/84, the developers felt that they had been given leave to argue a case that in the end would be much to their advantage, since presumably it would have led to substantial speculative gains. Had the proposal been granted permission, the lack of absolute certainty would have been a strength, not a weakness. The fact that both Foxley Wood and Tillingham Hall were refused was, however, taken as a weakness of the policy-making approach that preferred general statements of intent to detailed and possibly constraining allocations in plans. The decisions led to a renewed call for a greater degree of certainty in the development control process and for greater weight to be given to development plans and committed detailed policy. This experience explains the conciliatory attitude of the House Builders' Federation towards the planning system by the late 1980s.

Within the British system of development control, however, the ability to argue the case has by and large been seen as much a strength as a weakness by the development industry. Consider again the more recent case of a Tesco Superstore proposed for a key location at Meadowhead in southern Sheffield on what was a sports ground (Booth & Gibbs 1993). There was presumption against a development on playing fields, as a matter of both national and local policy, without a suitable alternative being found; the developers agreed to provide an alternative site. The alternative site was in the green belt, which again was against the intention of local policy; but the chosen site was derelict and the developers believed they could argue that it would be enhanced by being laid out as playing fields. Finally, there was an open question about how far the site of the superstore had amenity value (in itself a highly ambiguous concept). Tesco proceeded to apply for permission for its development in the absence of absolute certainty, in the belief that they had nevertheless a case to argue and in the knowledge that the gain to them if they were successful would be considerable. The fact that they were unsuccessful did not in this case devalue the general principle, perhaps because there were, in spite of the ambiguities, some clear parameters within which the case could be argued.

Earlier, we suggested that developers and the planning system appear to develop a kind of symbiosis. In Britain this is expressed as a need for a certainty that is nevertheless not too highly defined, allowing cases to be argued according to circumstance. If the relationship is symbiotic, British developers' attitudes may be a direct result of the particularities of the British system of development control. The question that follows is how developers respond in France and indeed anywhere where, in theory, zoning regulations confer a type of certainty absent in Britain. The fact seems to be that negotiation and agreement are as rife in zoning systems as in British development control. A comparative study of development control in Leiden and Oxford (Thomas et al. 1983: 133) had already begun to suggest that negotiation was an essential part of the control process in the heavily planned Netherlands. In particular, they noted how, in the expansion proposed for the district of Merenwijk, the plans that had been produced "served no useful purpose, expect to indicate that all participants in the planning process that the bargaining period [had] begun". Clearly, the only certainty that the Merenwijk extension plan had created was that development would be acceptable in the area, but none at all about the resulting form of the development itself. Three French cases in Lyon make the point abundantly clear. The first case concerns part of a major development in the suburban commune of Décines–Charpieu. Here the area had been defined in a ZAC in which large parcels would be developed by different housebuilders. On one of these parcels, which the developer coyly called Le Hameau des Cigales (Cicada hamlet), the regulations of the plan for the ZAC provided for a square with a small shopping centre and higher-density housing as a focus for the rest of the site, which would be single and semi-detached houses with gardens. The problem for the developer was that a decision to permit another group of shops on a site nearby made the shopping centre at Le Hameau des Cigales unviable, and the developer was anxious to set the regulations aside. Certainty at that level of detail was clearly irrelevant to the reality of the development at the moment it was proposed. To have insisted on the commercial centre would in all probability have ensured that the development would not have taken place at all.

The second case in another eastern suburb, St-Priest, concerned a plot of land for housing that consisted of a long strip in an area that was already substantially built up. The land in question had been zoned NA, that is land on which development would not be permitted, but only until such time as an appropriate scheme for servicing and infrastructure could be produced. The very fact of the zoning itself led to negotiations over the form the development would take, and under the general rubric of infrastructure, the mayor of St-Priest was able to get the developer to cede the main road frontage of the site for social housing. The final sticking point came with the length of the road that would serve the new housing. Here the regulations specified that no cul-de-sac should exceed 150m in length on the grounds of safety. This would have meant that the end of the site farthest from the existing main road would have been unusable. Hardly surprising, this was a certainty that the developer was not prepared to accept, and sought – with, it should be added, the collusion of the planning agency – to circumvent the letter of the regulations. The attempt was to no avail. The developer was forced to postpone development at the top quarter of the site, until the adjoining site could be developed and the cul-de-sac continued to form a loop, with access at both ends.

These two cases are of course about the detail of development, not the general principle. But a third case shows how both matters of principle and of detail may the subject of negotiation in the French system of zoning plans. This case concerns yet another housing development, Le Soleil Levant, in the commune of Vernaison, which this time concerns not a single housebuilder but a site developer laying out land as a *lotissement* (subdivision). The first issue in this case concerns the initial zoning of the land in the POS, which was NC, in other words, land that had to be protected from developments because of its agricultural value. The modification of the POS that was required before the development could take place seems to have been entirely routine for all that there was a policy intention to protect a green wedge along the banks of the River Rhône onto which the commune fronted. The site in question formed part of that green wedge. The re-zoning thus left free of developments the site's most conspicuous feature, the scarp slope running parallel to the river, which remained zoned NC.

With most of the site re-zoned as NA land – in other words land on which development would be acceptable once the scheme for servicing it could be agreed – the site developer was free to prepare a layout. In theory the regulations laid down with exactitude the form of development that would be given approval. However, in practice once again the developer sought to negotiate his way round three of the constraints. One had to do with lot size: it was found on inspection that some of the lots were substantially smaller than those allowed for detached houses in this area. The second had to do with the fact that some of the lots overlapped the boundary of the protected NC zoning on the scarp slope. The third was that, on part of the site above the scarp, building lots had been located in an *espace boisé classé* (classified woodland). This infringement was of a different order to the two others in that, although the authority that prepares the POS is required to identify woodland, once identified the woodland is subject to regulations in the *Code de l'urbanisme* itself, which effectively preclude development.

All these were in principle fixed limits about which there could be no uncertainty. All proved to be negotiable. The undersize plots would, the authorities informed the developer, be acceptable for semi-detached housing. In a classic bargaining stance, the developer agreed to modify some but not all of the plots concerned, on the grounds that the market would not stand more than a given number of semi-detached houses in this particular area. Infringement of the NC zoning on the scarp was resolved by agreeing that the zoning boundary had been drawn to the wrong contour line and that, in any case, building could be forbidden in those parts of the lots that were on the NC land. As for the *espace boisé classé*, everyone agreed that the identification, based on aerial photographs, was inappropriate. The land was scrub of little value, and therefore acceptable for building purposes.

The zoning and the regulations at Le Soleil Levant were thus not fixed limits at all but opening positions in the negotiations that then ensued. If there was any certainty, it was that the regulations provided a baseline from which the resulting development could depart. Just as much as in Britain, developers appeared to favour not absolute certainty but the chance of negotiating the best possible result.

Certainty and delay

There is another kind of certainty that has to do with process as much as with outcome. The main preoccupation of the debate about development control in Britain in the past two decades has been to do with delay rather than satisfactory outcomes. The wilful time-wasting of local planning authorities was the major problem that had to be confronted, as the evidence contained in the Expenditure Committee's report had made plain (House of Commons 1977). It took an US lawyer to suggest that the problem of delay was evidence that the British planning system was fundamentally flawed. McBride (1979) writing shortly after the Expenditure Committee's report had been published, argued that the essential problem was that the local plan could not provide an adequate base for develop-ment control because of the requirement that local authorities consider "other material considerations" in taking decisions. Decision-making was inevitably, therefore, slow and inconsistent. The remedy would be to adopt the US system of zoning ordinances that "influenced by the concept of 'rule of law' or 'admin-istrative due process' . . . seeks us to ensure more certainly, consistency and fair-ness to those affected by administrative decision-making, by limiting discretion, which is a mechanism of a requirement that such decisions must conform to clear, ascertainable standards, stated in advance" (ibid.: 58).

Leaving aside the questions of discretion and fairness, to which we shall return, McBride makes the assumption that the zoning produces swifter deci-sions. With regard to France if not the USA, the case is not proven. Certainty in terms of the proportion of applications of *permis de construire* that are refused, zoning and regulations do indeed appear to confer a degree of certainty that is absent in British development control. Comparing statistics from the early 1980s revealed that, whereas in the Britain the refusal rate was around 13 per cent, the figure in France was only 10 per cent (Booth 1989). In principle the *Code de l'urbanisme* lays down clear time limits within which decisions must be taken, which extend from two to a maximum of five months according to the type of development and the extent of consultation required. The limits are in practice closely adhered to because in the event of their being exceeded, an applicant receives a tacit permission to proceed. Yet the same comparison of processing statistics from the early 1980s of England and France showed no real difference in the percentage of applications determined within three months. Of course, these statistics must be treated with considerable caution, because the factors that influence processing time go well beyond the ease with which policy may be applied to individual cases. However, the fact remains that although applications for *permis de construire* are far more likely to be approved, they were not likely to be processed any faster, at least in the early 1980s.

Moreover, the question of delay and the time taken to process applications reveals anything but the full story. French case studies suggested that negotiations before an application was lodged were a major part of the process and that no application was lodged until it was in a state that was very likely to win its approval.

As we have already seen, those negotiations could be about negotiating departures from the regulations in the interest of realism or the nature of the site. Negotiations before an application is lodged are also a feature of British development control, of course, and have been seen variously as both a cure and a cause of delay. The Expenditure Committee could be concerned about the "additional stages" as they termed them, in the process that involved both pre- and post-application negotiations, central government itself has sometimes taken a different view: "effective consultation between the applicant and the planning authority – both before any formal application is made and afterwards – is crucial . . ." (DoE 1973). And the message was repeated in Circular 22/80 (DoE 1980). A focus on processing times alone thus obscures a good deal of the development control process and indeed of the unremunerative period for the developer between deciding to proceed with a development and the development being complete.

Case studies of housing development in the Yorkshire and Humberside region of Britain tried to look at the whole period between inception and completion of a project to determine what impact negotiations before applications were lodged actually had on the time taken. What emerged was that, although in some of the cases the processing times exceeded considerably the eight-week period for processing, determination of the planning applications nevertheless represented less than half (and in some cases as little as 11 per cent) of the total period. Conversely, a substantial part of the period was under the direct control of the developer. In particular, it was clearly open to the developer to choose at what stage to conclude negotiation and lodge an application. However, comparing the times taken between inception and development with the hypothetical case of a developer who chooses to appeal against the non-determination of the application, showed that there was not necessarily a great saving in time to be gained from negotiating. That in turn suggested that the purpose of negotiation was to optimize conditions under which the development would take place, or indeed ensuring that it would take place at all (Glasson & Booth 1992). So, the time taken to get a development from inception to completion is at least as much determined by the developer as it is by public authorities. Of course, it does not mean that time taken by local authorities to process applications does not rankle, because this is the one period over which developers may not have any control at all. In this respect, the French system of development control with fixed time limits and deemed permissions has a distinct advantage. Yet the process appears to be overall no quicker and the pre-application negotiations are even more critical than they are in Britain. The certainty that developers seem to be seeking is not so much the time it takes to elicit a decision but over the ability to secure the optimal decision at a moment of their choosing, not the controlling authority's.

Indeed, the overall message on certainty and developers seems to be that, although some certainty is desirable to minimize risk, developers choose to extend the time taken before construction starts in order to get the solution that most closely corresponds to their interests as they perceive them. Foxley Wood was infuriating for developers because government appeared to be saying that

95

the old constraints had been lifted in a way that could not be delivered in practice, and thus in the event created an uncertainty that went against the developers' interests. In this respect it is worth noting that the Tesco case in Sheffield is of a different order, because no implied leave to test the traditional constraints had been given, either locally or nationally. The developers knew the framework within which a decision would be taken and believed they could match the arguments.

Certainty and the decision-makers

Certainty and its absence are just as much a problem for decision-makers as for developers. The issue is above all else about ensuring that public policy can be maintained in dealing with the day-to-day pressure for development and that decision-makers have a clear and objective base for their decisions. Nevertheless, we have already noted that French and British systems of control are based on very different understandings of certainty and the impact of these different understandings needs exploration. In Britain, the overriding concern has been that the system should be flexible, not certain, and immediately the question arises as to how there can be any certainty in public policy at all, when flexibility becomes the ruling principle on which control is based. In France, it is certainty that is the preoccupation, and the question that follows must be how easily that certainty can be delivered.

France: upholding the law

In France, the codification of administrative law was essentially about providing a rational and objective set of criteria by which the country might be governed. Codified law was, therefore, about making the rights and duties of citizens clear. It was also about making sure that power could not be exercised arbitrarily. Thus, the codes also provided detailed advice to decision-makers – the administration – who were required to implement the laws and regulations that the codes contained. The *Code de l'urbanisme* is in that respect no different from any of the other codes that regulate public life in France. The trouble in development control has been that, in order to pre-empt increasingly difficult development problems, the tendency has been for the code and the POS to become ever more elaborate. Rules have proliferated and in practice have become harder and harder to apply. Inevitably that has led to a concerted effort to deregulate planning, not so much for the reasons that deregulation has been advanced in Britain, but to return the law to a kind of pristine simplicity where, once again, rights and duties would be abundantly visible to all the users of the code.

Several issues arise from this approach. The first is that of complexity. Elaboration is an attempt to try to create a greater degree of certainty by refining the regulations to a point at which they can address every eventuality. In practice, this seems to be productive of greater uncertainty. It becomes more and more difficult to see which rule might actually apply in a given circumstance, or how a given rule should be interpreted. Moreover, this problem seems to be endemic in zoning systems. The zoning ordinances of the USA have moved far from the simple tool that they were at the time of Euclid. We have already noted Cullingworth's (1994: 59) conclusions that "It is abundantly clear that zoning is not the rigid simple system of land use regulation that it is supposed to be . . . It is not simple: it is increasingly complex". Moseley's (1986) review of the Manhattan zoning ordinance demonstrates how difficult the interpretation of zoning can be in practice, requiring lengthy calculations on the part of both developers and city officials. At this level, zoning is far from clear for its users and cannot therefore easily point to a certain outcome. In Hong Kong, the same process is visible in the increasing complexity of the Outline Zoning Plans. So the continual refinement of regulations in the interest of achieving greater certainty may simply be counter-productive.

But how far do decision-makers really want certainty? Some of the elaborations that have been introduced into zoning plans reflect a rather different tendency. One of Bouyssou's criteria for "good" planning was that it should be stable and that the POS once elaborated would stand as a fixed point of reference for all its users. Yet in practice the POS has proved to be anything but stable. For example, Hocreitère (1991) noted that, in certain parts of France, revisions and modifications to POS in force were taking place more or less continuously, a problem that had acquired a much higher profile because of the many POS approved after 1983. One of the areas that Hocreitère singled out was Lyon and its *département* of Rhône. A detailed study of the *communauté urbaine* of Lyon revealed that Hocreitère was indeed right, and that, although some of the modifications were minor, significant changes were nevertheless taking place regularly (Booth & Stafford 1994). The particular difficulty here is that decisions may be deferred (*sursis à statuer*), pending the implementation of a change to the POS, or, that new rules may be applied in anticipation of the change. Auby (1987) is not alone in noting how this substitution of rules undermines the certainty that is their rationale. Clearly, in practice a higher premium is being placed upon managing the planning system to produce the best results, whatever these may appear to be, than in maintaining the certainty of the POS.

Part of the problem is of course to do with the nature of rules, which are by their nature concerned with fixed limits. Under some circumstances such limits are entirely appropriate to the nature of the planning task. But equally frequently they are not. The following cases make the point. The first is in the southeastern suburb of Lyon, Vénissieux, where in the mid-1980s the redevelopment of the old town centre, the remnant of the old medieval *bourg*, was taking place through the use of the ZAC procedure. A particular problem arose with development following the line of the old fortification, the Rue du Château. For the planner it directly concerned in the negotiations with the developer, relationships to scale were more important than finite geometric limits in the new development. The plan for the ZAC showed a boundary for the block that would maintain the existing street line adjacent to the church, but the boundary line had been shown so thick that it was impossible for the developer to interpret with any precision. The result was that the proposal was delayed when it was found to reduce the width of the street to a point at which it was impossible for fire engines to pass. For all that the urban design aspect of the development was not susceptible to simple regulatory control, the street width certainty did need to be subject to a fixed limit. This is a curious reversal of the more usual problems with regulatory systems, in which fixed limits appear to be a constraint to be overcome.

The other case is classic. A mayor of a commune in eastern Lyon sought a modification to the POS to allow a school extension project to proceed without the required 5 m setback from a main road. More than one interpretation of this change, which was in the event implemented, is possible. It could be seen as a pragmatic response to ensure that the project could go ahead; or it could have been simply special pleading by the mayor to favour a pet project. Either way, however, it raises the question as to what purpose the rule was designed to serve. If it was indeed an important measure of environmental protection, then its abandonment for a school and rest of the commune, was indefensible. If, however, as is more likely, it was the precise expression of an imprecise requirement that could in many cases be met in other ways, the rule had been inappropriate in the first instance. In both cases, rules were problematic and the regulatory system offered no real alternative. Certainty of outcome was thus fractured in the absence of the appropriate policy mechanism.

A final reflection on the problem of certainty comes with the example with rural communes' attitudes to control. As we have seen, decentralization of powers to local authorities in France was linked to the preparation of POS. Once the POS had been prepared, the commune took over responsibility for processing and determining *permis de construire*. In practice, central government recognized that, in spite of the implicit intention, universal coverage by POS was unlikely. So, too, small rural communes were by no means equally enthusiastic about preparing a POS, which were regularly stated to be "too constraining". Part of the reason was that mayors of small communes were frightened by the new responsibilities that they would acquire by having a POS; part, that POS were simply too detailed for the needs of the enormous numbers of communes where "the rhythm of development is slow" (Minstère de l'Équipement, du Logement, de l'Aménagement du territoire et des Transports 1987). A mayor ran the risk of having his or her hands tied by the certainties that the POS would confer. On the other hand, without a POS control was left in the hands of the state, and specifically the DDE, who then applied the national urban regulations in the code in determining applications for *permis de construire*. More particularly there was the difficult issue of deciding what constituted the built-up area of the commune to which development would be limited in the absence of a POS. The way around these difficulties was the use a document that set out for the commune concerned an agreement with the *DDE* on how the *RNU* would be applied. This document, the *modalités d'application du règlement national urbain* (*MARNU*: method of implementing the national urban regulations) in practice allowed a certain amount of leeway on the *règle de constructibilité limitée* and provided a measure of certainty about how the general rules of the code would be used in the event. All in all, it has proved in a minority of communes to be a useful tool. It increases certainty about decisions but without carrying the legal constraints of the *POS* or the threat of new responsibilities. The process also becomes more certain. The *MARNU* provides a fixed point of reference for decisions that need no longer appear simply to be taken at the whim of the mayor or on the diktat of the state services (Booth 1988, 1994).

Britain: the limits to flexibility

France has tried to constrain the hand of the decision-maker by a system of *POS* with zones and regulations, in order to ensure that everyone is certain about development possibilities; Britain has gone in an entirely different direction. The first post-war system of development plans were rejected because they were too constraining and insufficiently responsive to development needs. And in the early 1980s the Conservative government was at pains to stress the discretion available to local authorities in promoting development necessary for economic growth. Author after author has stressed the need for flexibility and responsiveness in the planning system (see, for example, Keeble 1964, Brindley et al. 1989, Thornley 1991). However, there is a double problem in this attitude. On the one hand, emphasizing the freedom that local authorities had to take decisions was very much a two-edged sword. Local authorities were quite as likely to take decisions that could not be justified in the terms of the thrust of central government policy as they were to take decisions that did. In the end it was not at all helpful that, by 1988, still only 18 per cent of the country was covered by local plans (DOE 1988), because builders could complain that local planning authorities were too often using their discretion to refuse rather than to permit development. There was clearly an important case for getting local authorities to commit themselves to policy by requiring them to prepare local plans for the whole of their areas, reintroduced in the Planning and Compensation Act 1991 after a gap of 23 years. This new-found enthusiasm for plan-making was not thus a conversion to the virtues of regulation by the state, but a way of creating certainties that were seen as having been eroded by local government activity. In general terms, local authorities themselves welcomed the new requirement. In the first place, and probably most importantly, the return to what is now referred to as a "plan-led system" of planning suggested that planning had once again became a respectable activity and not a bureaucratic hindrance. But it also meant that local authorities could foresee a greater degree of certainty in their decision-making. No longer was there the risk that decisions taken in accordance with local policy would be set aside on appeal in the light of generalized criteria contained in Circulars, something that appeared to be an increasing threat by the mid-1980s (Davies et al. 1986).

In one way, then, Britain seems to be moving in the same direction as France, which, by insisting on a *POS* before communes could assume new powers of development control, had wanted to ensure that local power was not unbridled. But the analogy cannot be taken very far. Section 54a of the Town and Country Planning Act 1990 that now makes the development plan the first consideration in the determination of planning applications is essentially enigmatic. What ministers have done is to interpret it as implying a policy presumption in favour of development that is in accordance with the plan, something that, as a matter of policy, they are entirely entitled to do (Grant 1991). However, such case law as it appears so far does not suggest that much has changed. Other material considerations may still outweigh policy contained in a plan (Purdue 1994).

The return to plan-making is not the only way in which the British government has tried to increase the degree of certainty in decision-making by local planning authorities. A classic means for doing so from the very beginnings of a discretionary system of planning was through the Circulars in which central government interpreted the duties and responsibilities of successive Acts of Parliament for local authorities. In effect, these became policy directives, whose intention was to give a clear lead and provide criteria against which development control decisions could be judged nationally. Nor could local planning authorities afford to ignore the advice Circulars offered. In the event of an appeal, inspectors would – and did – consider a local authority's decisions in the light of relevant Circulars, and jurisprudence had long since held that Circulars could indeed be material to a decision. If the French case suggests that absolute certainty (at any rate in the form of regulations) is neither attainable nor desired by decision-makers, the British experience shows that development control systems do not operate easily in the absence of markers. The question is not just one of central government trying to impose its will on local authorities, it is at least as much to do with local authorities wanting to create order and the decisions they have to take.

Landowners and certainty

Landowners' desire for certainty in knowing what development may be permitted on the land they own is in some ways close to that of developers. On the one hand, they do need to know what limits will be imposed upon them, but while being expected to negotiate to maximize their gain. On the other hand there are other issues at stake that have an important influence on the nature of planning control. Perhaps the key question is to what extent there are constitutional rights to landownership. In France, the starting point is the fact that the Constitution itself grants the right to own land: *le droit inviolable et sacré*. Of course, as Comby (1989) pointed out, this right has long since ceased to be inviolable and the absolute right to property has been replaced by a right to property within the confines of other law. Nevertheless, it forms the starting point for any discussion about control of development in France. Significantly, too, it means that zoning plans in the *POS* are about establishing exactly what rights landowners do have. The *POS* itself confers these rights, which makes any departure from the original plan, however carried out, a threat in constitutional terms as well as in terms of policy.

Planning control and land values

This is not the whole story, however. Another issue of signal importance to the landowners is the question of the value of the land. We have argued that developers have looked to the planning system to create order in the land market. So too, landowners have increasingly used the planning system to ascertain the value of the land that they own. In Britain the issue was at the outset cast in terms of the question of compensation and betterment. The story of how the problem was resolved goes beyond the scope of this book to recount in detail (but see Cox 1984). However, the essential problem that faced the emerging planning system was that, if as a result of a plan a landowner was deprived of the right to develop, was compensation not due? And if that were the case, how could you be sure that, but for the plan, the land would in fact have been developed? The question posed by betterment was the reverse: if the state had created its values by virtue of the plans that it had drawn up, was it not also right that the state should recover the value created? Although Britain has never effectively resolved the question of recovering betterment values, the question of what price a parcel of land might fetch, was in effect dealt with by the 1947 Town and Country Planning Act, which extinguished inherent development rights in favour of a universal system of control that conferred a right to develop only once the planning permission had been granted. Thus, seeking a valid planning permission became the only effective way to establish land values, even if the development plan might give an indication of the likely potential. But the plan could not do so alone, because other material considerations might dictate a specific solution. This inevitably placed great pressure on the development control process to deliver quickly and favourably, since certainty is only delivered with the planning permission. This makes plain not only the irritation with the apparently wilful or "political" decision-making, but also the preoccupation with delay.

In Hong Kong it is the government as ground landlord that discovered an interest in planning control as a means of fixing the premiums it could charge on leases. The interests of the government and developers tend both to favour planning and to oppose it. On the one hand, since the 1970s at least, the government has been acutely aware of the value of the development industry to the territory's economy as a whole, and therefore concerned to ensure that development could proceed with a minimum of interference. On the other hand, both sides need certainty if the industry is to function. Developers need to know what they can do

101

with the leases they purchase from the government, and the government needs to know what it can charge them. But as we noted, there is also the effect on land values of development on adjoining sites. Developers and the government-as–landowner need to be certain about what may happen across an area and not just on a given site. In a rather different kind of way from the French *POS*, the Hong Kong Outline Zoning Plans are also about rights: the right to build and the right to see land values protected.

Protecting intangible values

Again, it is in the protection of neighbourhood land values through the use of zoning ordinances that landowners in the USA have found certainty. Babcock & Siemon (1985) recount a series of case studies that feature the fight by landowners to protect their property from the effects of new development. The values that embattled citizens of the Tuxedo, New York State, Palm Beach or Sanibel island in Florida were fighting for were as much intangible as monetary and were essentially about maintaining a privileged or sensitive environment. The most acute case, however, is that of Mount Laurel, in which a suburb of Philadelphia was challenged for doing what other communities had done for some while: using zoning as a way of excluding the poor and black populations of the city, establishing themselves in the area through what Babcock & Siemon describe as "A veritable trunkful of techniques" (ibid.: 209). In 1975 these were ruled by the New Jersey Supreme Court as unacceptable. Strikingly, however, in a second decision that reinforced the earlier one, the Court set out ten policy considerations, together with a detailed footnote on how in future municipalities should calculate their obligation to provide low-cost homes according to a particularly complex formula.

The rights of third parties

Certainty in the knowledge of the value of your landholding, and the certainty of knowing that the value will not be adversely affected by the way in which your neighbours use their land, is thus a major factor in the acceptance of zoning. This, then, takes us directly to the question of third-party rights and the extent to which certainty is needed and is possible in the development control process for those affected by development but not directly involved in it. The Babcock & Siemon cases from the USA aptly illustrate citizen power and the use of the courts to maintain the quality of the environment through the legal right to challenge or uphold a pattern of zoning. In France, the zoning and regulations of the *POS* might be expected to work in the same way. A fundamental principle of codified administrative law is that it allows third parties the right to challenge the decisions of the administration. This means that the zoning of a *POS* may be contested in law, and decisions on *permis de construire* are also open to contest after the decision is taken. Indeed, in France there is a formal four-month period in which such a challenge may be made after the decree granting a permission has been issued. In principle, this ensures that third parties have a considerable degree of certainty: nothing can be done that is not specifically sanctioned in the *POS* or a regulation in the code.

France: third-party rights and practice

The reality is not quite so simple, as the following case study from the commune of Vernaison shows. At the edge of commune was the depot of a haulage firm, Transports Griset, in a partly rural area surrounded by a scattering of houses that formed the hamlet of Le Pellet. The depot had been established in 1948 and had grown from a small family firm with two trucks to a sizeable enterprise with a fleet of 150 vehicles and 200 employees. To accommodate that growth, the depot had been enlarged by stages, but it was the most recent extension that reveals how zoning does not always deliver the certainty that third parties expect. In 1985 Transports Griset, still run by the founder's son, applied to extend the depot once again, and to lay out a considerable area of concrete hardstanding. Local residents from Le Pellet vigorously opposed this latest extension and formed themselves into a local amenity group.

On the face of it, there should have been little difficulty in opposing the application. Although the Griset depot had long pre-dated the present system of plans and control, the *POS* for the southwestern sector of the Lyon conurbation had been approved in 1982. The depot had been included in a developed zone, classified U in the *POS*, but allocated for low-density residential development in which flats might exceptionally be permitted. There was no zoning in this part of Vernaison for commerce or industry, and much of the area outside the residential zoning for Le Pellet was reserved for agriculture. However, there was an important clause that made an exception for extensions to existing industrial or commercial premises. Thus:

> the extension, transformation or reconstruction of industrial or craft enterprises may be permitted on the following conditions:
>
> - that they are accompanied by a reduction in the danger, the inconvenience or the unhealthiness of an enterprise;
> - that they do not exacerbate the general conditions of the location of the enterprise in the environment." (Agence d'Urbanisme de la Communauté Urbaine de Lyon 1982, Règlement, Article 2).

For a variety of reasons that did not appear to bear on the planning merits of the case, the mayor of the commune was concerned to approve the case and the technical staff of the Agence d'Urbanisme did not oppose the mayor's wish. The decision was not a legal one because the *POS* specifically offered an option to determine the case outside the general rules of the zone.

Although there is an open question about how far the decision on the latest extension to the depot actually made things worse for residents of Le Pellet, there are two significant points in the case about the certainties that the residents looked for and the extent to which the system could deliver them. The first point to note is that, although in principle *POS* offered a clear view of future use, the let-out clause for existing industrial premises immediately clouded the clarity. The exception introduced a new criterion ("not exacerbating the general conditions . . .") that was not given any finite measure against which it could be judged. The decision depended on a judgement of the decision-maker. The plan itself could not offer the certainty that the residents wanted. The second point has to do with process. The residents had two options in influencing the outcome of the application. They could try to lobby the mayor and persuade him that a permission would affect the environment, but the pressures on the mayor to accept the extension were greater than a desire to placate part of his electorate. The law allowed them no formal right to participate in the making of the decision. The other option was to contest in law the decision once taken by appealing to the administrative courts. In the event, the residents also failed to take this remedy largely through a failure to cope with the administrative complexity of lodging an appeal. But even if they had done so, there was no guarantee of their success. The decision was to all intents and purposes within the scope of the regulations. A judge could conceivably have ruled that there was *erreur manifeste d'appréciation,* in that the authorities had failed to assess the full impact of the extension, but such an outcome was by no means certain.

Two factors eroded the apparent certainties of the *POS* and the system of *permis de construire* in this case. First, there was the option offered by the regulations of the *POS* that did not specify the parameters within which a decision could be taken. Secondly, there was no means by which the effects of the extension could be properly evaluated. Both the grounds for the decision and the process by which it was taken were inherently uncertain for the residents because they were essentially covert. Residents could only explain the decision in terms of money having changed hands. The apparent strength of the redress offered by codified administrative law had failed them in this case.

Britain: the right to object

The case of the Tesco superstore at Meadowhead, Sheffield offers an interesting contrast. Here, there was no *POS* to identify appropriate land uses; indeed, there was no formally approved plan at all, because Sheffield's Unitary Development Plan (UDP) was still only in draft form. The only guide was a bundle of older policy documents at the local level, which aimed to secure the replacement of existing playing fields on development, and a generalized national policy in the form of a Planning Policy Guidance Note (DOE 1989), which, among other things, stressed the amenity value of open space. At the outset, the residents who objected strenuously to the proposal, had no certainty that their objections had any real foundations, given the willingness of Tesco to replace the playing fields and provide open space for public use on the site itself. Like the residents of Le Pellet, their first option was to lobby their locally elected representatives. This they did with rather greater effect, both because of better organization and because of greater numbers. There was little doubt that resident pressure, rather than the advice of their officers, led the City Council to refuse the application for development. However, there was the second test in the form of the inevitable appeal that Tesco lodged against the Council's decision. The certainty of the first victory was provisional, but in the event there, too, residents were able to make a case that was vindicated by the Inspectors' decision to uphold the refusal of permission (Booth & Gibbs 1994).

Neither in principle nor in practice did the state of planning policy at the time of the case offer residents any certainty about the future of an open space that they regarded as important to them. But they did have a measure of security in the process itself, even if they did not recognize the fact until after the event. First, they had a right to make objections to the original proposal, which the City Council was obliged to consider in its decision. Secondly, they also had a *de facto* right to be heard when the decision went to appeal. The basis for a decision that was every bit as ambiguous as the basis for a decision in the Griset case was nevertheless subject to open presentation in a way that left residents satisfied that, whatever the outcome, justice had somehow been done. Had the City Council granted permission for the superstore, the residents would, if anything, been worse off than their counterparts in Le Pellet. Until the inquiry itself, the people of Meadowhead believed that the process was unfolding in secrecy, without their being able to influence events. Even if they did not see the process as corrupt, they saw it as covert, in spite of their right in law to object. A decision to approve would have been virtually incontestable.

Conclusion: the need for certainty and the availability of certainty

The kind and extent of certainty that different actors need from systems of planning control are evidently varied: certainty is not perceived in the same way by everyone involved. The first point to make is that plans and planning control of whatever kind are seen as important in creating certainty. Developers are averse to risk and they favour systems that allow them to take decisions that are not wholly unconstrained. There appears to be a broad consensus across the different systems of control touched on here. Zoning ordinances in the USA caught on with the developers as well as with home-owners and environmentalists, because of the order they brought to the land market. The British House Builders' Federation has favoured plans for much the same reasons. But to assume that developers want absolute certainty, and thus for every aspect of development to be fixed in advance, appears to be false.

In Britain, the debate on planning has always been dominated by the concept of flexibility. There is therefore no surprise in finding in the Yorkshire and Humberside case studies that housebuilders favoured negotiations with the local authorities who were prepared to apply standards flexibly (Glasson & Booth 1992). In the USA and France, whose zoning systems apparently leave nothing to chance, there is, however, equally a desire to go beyond the apparently fixed limits of the regulations and ordinances. A degree of uncertainty allows for the negotiation of an optimal result.

So, developers seek to limit uncertainty while seeking to ensure that local authorities' fixed requirements are not the last word on development proposals. For local authorities, too, the quest for certainty is not simple. The Tesco case in Sheffield led the city planners to refine their policies on open space as a way of ensuring a greater degree of precision in future about the objectives they were trying to achieve through the control of development on playing fields. They were moving to limit their own uncertainty to ease the process of maintaining policy in respect of particular decisions. Yet two tendencies tend to limit this quest for certainty. First, the search for ever greater precision appears to lead not to greater certainty but to – in Bouyssou's (1986) words – "a return to Byzantium" in which rules become ever more difficult to apply. Secondly, for planning authorities, the leeway to negotiate is significant. At Meadowhead and Vernaison, the authorities were all prepared to negotiate to secure the benefit of the development to them. At St-Priest and Bron, the authorities pushed against limits that they themselves had imposed. As for developers, parameters for their decision-making are clearly important to increase certainty and reduce risk, but rule-making may in the end defeat its own objectives.

The fundamental question here has to do with the nature of rules and the extent to which rule-making is possible for something as inherently uncertain as planning. Jowell (1973) comments that rules are effective in dealing with problems that simply involve a yes-or-no response, or when there is a clear objective shared by all participants. They work badly if the problem is essentially a multi-polar one. Thus, in the Vénissieux case, access by safety service vehicles was possible only if a minimum street width was maintained and this was clearly susceptible to a precise regulation whose absence merely served to delay the development. Much the same could be said about the classified woodland on the site for Le Soleil Levant. If there was general agreement that woodland must be protected at all costs, the precise regulations of the *Code de l'urbanisme* were entirely appropriate. What was flawed was the manner of identifying the area of woodland on the site itself. By contrast, the objective of a fixed limit for the cul-de-sac at St-Priest or the set-back requirement at Bron seem far from clear and could perhaps have been met in other ways. The same must be true of the other regulations that were contentious at Le Soleil Levant. Because the objectives were not clear, either for plot sizes or for the boundaries of the undevelopable, NC, zones, the limits became negotiable in a way that the legislation had not intended. This point has already been made in the British context by Woodford et al. (1976), who argued that fixed limits such as density standards all too readily become proxies for real objectives that may be in conflict.

Two things emerge from this. The first is that a clear expression of objectives with performance criteria attached may be a better way for policy to be expressed. Rules and fixed limits may be some of the criteria that are used, but they will not stand alone. The second is that there has to be a process for ensuring an evaluation of these criteria as they apply to given cases. Residents at Le Pellet were not merely denied any certainty of achieving a desired outcome, they also lacked any means of putting the appropriateness of the decision to the test, unlike their counterparts at Meadowhead. And even at Meadowhead, residents were unsure as to how a decision would be reached until the inquiry. Certainty of process is clearly of considerable importance.

However, there is a further issue that this chapter has touched upon. It is that developers clearly do not want total certainty, nor would it appear from the regularity of the changes being made to POS, do the decision-makers. The insistence in Britain on the need for flexibility is clearly a reflection of the same desire. However, this desire to circumvent absolute certainty takes us into a new area, that of the power to take decisions and the discretion that is available to those that hold that power. This forms the theme of the next chapter.

CHAPTER 6
Flexibility, discretion and accountability

Having been educated as a planner in Britain and having had direct experience of practice in more than one local authority, I was nurtured in the belief that flexibility was the most important ingredient in a successful planning system. Flexibility was important in a technical sense in that planning was clearly an uncertain process, and allowance had to be made to accommodate the unforeseen. It was important, too, in helping to oil the wheels of the administrative mechanism that kept the technical process going. As students shortly after the new system of structure and local plans had been introduced, my contemporaries and I could laugh at the rigidities of the 1947 development plans. Only when I came to investigate the French planning system did I begin to see that not everyone held flexibility in quite the esteem that I did. The desire to make changes, the ranges of options available to decision-makers, all of which seemed quite natural, appeared to evoke considerable disquiet, at least in some quarters, in France.

Discretionary power

In thinking about flexibility as simply some kind of convenient lubrication without which no planning process could work, I began to realize that I had obscured a rather more fundamental issue. Flexibility in planning control does of course imply a discretion to take a decision in the light of circumstances; those who have discretion to act are those who have power. Any discussion of flexibility in planning takes us to the heart of the debates on how the modern state does, or should, conduct its affairs. Lawyers, political scientists and those involved in social welfare issues have all contributed to the debate. Before looking at the specific question of discretionary power in planning control, some discussion of the wider theoretical background is necessary.

Defining discretion

Initial definitions are offered by many authors, but Jowell's reference to the "room for decisional manoeuvre possessed by the decision-maker" (Jowell 1973: 178) and the rather fuller definition by Ham & Hill (1985: 4) are helpful: "A public officer has discretion whenever the effective limits of his power make him free to make a choice among the public courses of action or inaction".

Jowell notes, too, that discretion "is rarely absolute and rarely absent" (ibid.: 178) and his words are echoed by others. But to conclude that discretion is about choice in decision-making and that there is much of it about hardly advances the argument very far. There must be some sympathy with Smith's (1981: 60) view that "the apparent supposition that we can settle upon a definition before research beings . . . [is] unhelpful".

One way forwards is to try to define discretion by antithesis. Thus, for Davis (1971) writing about the problem of discretion in the US system of administration as a whole, discretion is the antithesis of law, and the role of law must be to contain unbridled discretion. This attitude is reflected in the considerable body of literature that opposes discretion to rules, and Ham & Hill note that the discussion of one sooner or later involves the discussion of the other. In this context, the way that British planners have favoured discretion (e.g. Davies 1980, Thomas et al. 1983) is by no means shared by those involved in other public services. Noble (1981) shows how the Housing Corporation formulated rules that were in practice widely departed from, but Bradshaw (1981) reports that the Family Fund increasingly moved towards formulating instructions to introduce consistency in its decision-making. Discretion may be necessary to free decision-makers from the inflexibility of rules; rules will be necessary to ensure that discretion is not merely a matter of personal whim that leads to injustice and reduces the possibility of redress. Discretion and rules are not merely opposites, they are interdependent.

Yet even this conceptualization is limiting. To suggest that rules and discretion are opposite ends of a sliding scale is to present them as a similar order of phenomenon. Dworkin's (1979) image of discretion suggests something rather different:

> The concept of discretion is at home in only one sort of context; when someone is charged with making decisions set by a particular authority . . . Discretion, like the hole in the doughnut, does not exist except as an area left by a surrounding belt of restriction. It is therefore a relative concept. It always makes sense to ask 'Direction under what standards?' or 'Discretion as to what authority?'" (Dworkin 1977: 31).

There are two main points to make about this quotation. The first is that it reinforces Jowell's assertion that discretion is rarely absolute, but must operate within limits. The second is that it suggests that discretion is not so much a thing in itself as a shorthand term for dealing with ways in which the power to take decisions is allocated, the criteria by which decisions are taken, and the mechanisms by which decision-makers account for their actions. Thus, as Adler & Asquith (1981) observe, discretionary power is a direct reflection of power relationships within society as a whole.

The literature makes it clear that discretion is available in a variety of forms. There is, first of all, a distinction that both Bull (1980) and Donnison make between judgement that is the simple interpretation of rules" and discretion in which rules "give specific functionaries in particular situations the responsibility to make such decisions as they think fit" (cited by Ham & Hill 1984: 149). That is then further refined by Bull, writing about the British system of supplementary benefits. He makes a distinction between what he called agency and officer discretion. In the former, the agency – in the case of supplementary benefits, a central commission – has discretionary powers conferred upon it by Parliament. The latter originates from the activities of individual officers and is subject to control, if at all, only at the local level. Bull then further breaks down officer discretion into the discretion implied by the interpretation of rules, taking decisions where rules are deemed inappropriate, and departing from rules. Bull cautions that to confuse agency and officer discretion is to blur two quite separate problems:

> My concern is that the failure to distinguish between these different levels and types of activities can contribute to a confusion of issues: the extent to which Parliament should leave scope for agencies and/or officials to exercise discretion in exceptional circumstances; and whether and how checks can be imposed on the *inevitable* power of officers at the point of delivery to make a judgement about claims by their fellow human beings for that service" (Bull 1980: 68).

Adler & Asquith make another distinction, this time between professional and administrative discretion. Professionals, they argue, are prime examples of discretionary actors who are "subject to particularly weak forms of accountability and control". They can justify their use of discretion by laying claims to "esoteric professional knowledge" and have retained the power to act "through the development of powerful forms of occupation control" (1981: 13). The power wielded by professionals is thus great and the exercise of what is often referred to as their professional judgement is accorded high status. Administrative discretion, on the other hand, is low status, characteristically constrained by rules or guidelines, but because administrators do not share in a professional subculture, it is more likely to be distorted by personal ideology. It is also more readily criticized and controlled. So discretion may not simply be a question of institutional as against individual freedom of action, but may also depend on the characteristics of the actor.

Although none of this discussion stems from an analysis of town planning – social welfare and administrative law are the two key areas in which the debate has been located – the applicability to the control of development of the concepts discussed above is obvious. The freedoms and constraints offered by the law, the decisions of individual actors in the public sector and the relationship between administrative and technical expertise are all involved. Before moving on to discuss how discretionary power is used and contained in British and French development control, two particular areas of activity in which discretion is an issue require further exploration. The first is to do with the extent of discretionary power in local government. The second takes up the theme of discretion in administrative law. Both have a critical bearing on the control of development.

Discretion and local government

If to discuss discretion generally takes us into the vexed debate on social welfare and individual rights, to discuss local authority discretion is to broach the equally convoluted field of central–local relations. Much of this debate would appear to be about whether and to what extent local government can be autonomous (Rhodes 1980). But in whatever terms it is couched, the debate is essentially about Bull's agency discretion and has little to do with discretion for the individual.

A convenient starting point might be the model of British local government that Lagroye & Wright (1979) offer as a contrast to the model they perceive for French local government. In referring to it as a "residual domain", they imply that there are areas of service and welfare provision that the central state has regarded as being better handled by local government. This Lagroye & Wright contrast with the "conceded domain" of French local government, where the central state has grudgingly given partial control to local authorities over activities in which the state nevertheless retains a strong contact.

First of all, the idea that local government has an equal role with central government, accorded to it by Parliament, suggests in Rhodes' words a view of central and local government being in partnership, which in turn leads to a view that local government is or should be essentially autonomous within the constraints imposed by Acts of Parliament. Such a view has led to what Rhodes can describe as the "conventional wisdom" that local government autonomy has been eroded by successive stages, through directive and financial control, and local authorities have been reduced to being mere agents of central government. Rhodes argues that the conventional wisdom is not supported by the facts and that, if the concept of complete autonomy was something of a myth, so too was the idea that central control was removing all local authorities' discretion to act.

The first point that Rhodes makes is that, so far from being easily described by clear concepts such as "partnerships", "residual domain" and *ultra vires*, the relationship between the two levels of government is essentially ambiguous and confused, and multi- rather than unidimensional. Thus, a local authority does not deal with central government as a single phenomenon, but with a multiplicity of departments, agencies and quangos. Moreover, these relationships are mediated by policy committees that straddle institutional boundaries and what Rhodes calls the "national community of local government" to produce a very complex structure. It is hardly surprising that central government finds it much harder to control local government than popular imagination would suppose. The real problem for local government, Rhodes argued, was that local authorities were forced to operate in an atmosphere of considerable uncertainty, which made long-term strategy difficult if not impossible (Rhodes 1980, 1986).

The second point that Rhodes makes is that local authorities have never been fully autonomous. At the same time, the multiplicity of relationships between the tiers of government, and central government's need to rely upon local authorities to implement policy, offer local government considerable leeway to negotiate, and in negotiating to exercise discretion. In his study of transport policy in South Yorkshire, Howells (1983) exemplifies the essentially ambiguous character of the local authorities' relationship with central government and the way in which that relationship was in a state of constant evolution born of the interdependence of both levels of government in making policy and implementing it. And even in the 1980s Rhodes argues that apparent directive control by central government has been offset by evasive action by local authorities, which has resulted in unforeseen impacts on other policy areas. This holds true, even if the relationship between the actors is equal, as the state's "monopoly of legislative resources" led Rhodes to recognize that they were often not:

> In short, there is a tension between interdependence and the exercise of executive authority and analysis must focus on the interaction between the two. Neither bargaining nor control is the appropriate focus even when the relationship is asymmetric." (Rhodes 1986: 6).

In this light it is clear that, even if we were to retain the more simplistic "partnership" and "agency" models of local–central relations, and to persist in arguing that there was a shift towards local authorities as agents of the state, local authorities would not thereby lose all their discretionary power. Indeed, organization theory posits that the very act of delegating results in the transfer of at least some discretionary power (Ham & Hill 1984) and that transfer must presumably occur between organizations as between individuals. The point is reinforced by the practice of the present British government not to make local authorities mere ciphers under the control of the state, but to circumvent them altogether by transferring powers to other bodies or by giving ministries direct responsibility for what have hitherto been local authority functions.

The messages that come across from this largely British discussion of local government and discretion must nevertheless have a wider application. The first must be that, in a unitary state, local authorities cannot be wholly autonomous; they will work for better or worse in a context of national policy, for which part of their function is to be the implementing agency. The second is that, if local authorities in a unitary state are never wholly autonomous, they can to a greater or lesser extent act with discretion because their relationship with the state is one of interdependence and not simple subservience: there is room for manoeuvre. The real question is how that discretion is used and what constraints there are upon its use. The third message is that local authorities are likely to have many different types of relationship with central government and that these will modify over time. The specific dynamics of a given relationship and the specific context within which the actors operate will be of paramount importance in knowing the extent of the discretionary power available and the likely outcome of negotiation.

Discretion and administrative law

If the issue of discretion in local government is really to do with the relative freedom of local authorities in relation to the central state, seen from a legal perspective the issue is about whether there should be administrative discretion at all, and, if there should, how the law might then control it. The origins of this debate lie ultimately with the nineteenth-century theorist Dicey, who argued that there was no such thing in England as administrative law and that "the state possessed no exceptional powers and . . . individual public servants were responsible to the ordinary courts of the land for their use of statutory powers" (Harlow & Rawlings 1984: 15). Dicey is therefore the progenitor of what Harlow & Rawlings call "red light theories" of administrative law that see the power of state as arbitrary and something to be resisted through legal control. It is from this attitude that modern calls for a return to the rule of law derive in relation to specific acts of administration that are perceived as arbitrary.

Adler & Asquith (1981), following Tay & Kamenka, regard this desire for legality as presenting a crisis in the law itself. Lawyers raised in the tradition of *gesellschaft* law based on "atomic individualism and private interests" find it hard to cope with administrative law, in which private interest is often subordinate to the achievement of public policies. The argument goes further that *gesellschaft* law is unable to deal with the discretion wielded by modern government, and the return to the rule of the law produces procedural rights without necessarily tackling "basic social and structural inequalities" (pp. 20–21).

However, there is a rather different view encompassed by what Harlow & Rawlings call "green light theories" of administrative law, which recognizes that discretion was inevitable, even desirable for the operation of modern administration, but a problem remained about how to make the exercise of discretionary power more accountable. For such commentators as Wade, administrative law is necessary to ensure that the executive conforms "to the principles of liberty and fair dealing" (Ham & Hill 1948: 159). Davis (1971) believed the answer lay in the legalization of the administrative process by developing administrative rules rather than relying upon adjudication through the courts to control and to create policy. Rules are fair because they are explicit, but the limits of their effectiveness had to be recognized. Davis thus goes a stage beyond what he describes as the "extravagant version of the rule of law "which argues that only the law can provide certainty and justice for the individual. First, the rule of law does not in fact provide that certainty, in that judges themselves act with discretion according to circumstances. Secondly, Davis recognized it would be incompatible with the needs of modern administration. But his analysis rests on the need to distinguish between necessary and unnecessary discretion, and then that necessary administrative discretion can only be confirmed by rules.

Jowell's (1973) analysis takes the discussion further. We have already noted that he recognized the necessity for, and the ambiguity of, discretion: he proceeds to examine how, and how far, the law can in fact control it. For Jowell, there are in effect two legal means: by "legalization", or the formulation of explicit rules for action, and "judicialization", or the subjecting of decisions to the adjudicative procedures of courts of law. In examining these two processes, Jowell argues there must be two criteria by which they should be judged. First, at a strategic level, it is important to know "whether legal techniques will prove effective means to achieve given ends" (ibid.: 183). Secondly, it is necessary to know whether in fact the task in hand is susceptible to legal control.

In considering the question of certainty, we have already enquired whether rules are appropriate to planning problems and do indeed make the process of control more certain. From the point of view of discretionary power, Jowell notes that rules bring the benefits of clarity and accountability to administration, aid efficiency and serve to protect individual administrators. On the other hand, they may prove rigid and encourage legalistic behaviour. Adjudication similarly has strengths in allowing participation in the decision-making process and by requiring the decision-maker to give a justification on the basis of a declared principle, rule or standard. It also allows the "incremental elaboration of laws on the basis of a case-by-case treatment of issues" (ibid.: 198). Yet adjudication may confer procedural rights without substantive rights, and the focus on an individual's rights may make it difficult to generalize for the administrative task from the particular case; to that extent, adjudication is inferior to rule-making.

There are three observations to be made about this argument as it stands. The first is that the formulation of rules does not of itself presume that decisions will also be the subject of adjudication, although decisions subject to adjudication may be justified in the light of a rule. The second is that adjudication always requires the justification of decisions, but by reference in principle to more than just a legal code. The third observation to make is that, once a rule is in place, it may avoid arbitrary decision-making, but the process by which rules themselves are made may not necessarily be free of arbitrariness. How rules are made in a legalized system of administration will need to be scrutinized; so, too, will the other means by which decisions are justified.

The argument cannot end there, however; we need to consider Jowell's criterion for assessing legal control:

> What are the limits of rule-governed conduct? The essential limit arises as a corollary of the fact that a rule is a general direction applicable to a number of 'like' situations that may arise in future . . . The corollary therefore of the impersonal nature of rules is that they are unsuited to the guidance of situations where the action to be controlled is non-recurring. (ibid.: 202).

Jowell is thus departing from commentators such as Davis (1971), who see rule-making as the only antidote to unfettered discretion by affirming that rules will help in assisting only with certain tasks. Standards, on the other hand, are means of measuring flexibility in policy-making because they require "in addition to the finding of a fact . . . a qualitative appraisal of the fact, in terms of its probable consequences or moral justification" (ibid.: 203). They clearly do allow for a greater responsiveness to a particular circumstance, and can adapt to changes over time. The application of a standard to a specific problem would thus appear to be an essentially discretionary act on the part of the administrator, but one that becomes susceptible to adjudication because its basis is clear. Standards nonetheless can only be used, like rules, where the problems recur.

Legal control not only becomes difficult in dealing with unique problems, it becomes difficult, too, where the problem is of the kind that Jowell, following Polanyi, calls polycentric. Jowell argues that adjudication deals invariably with "yes/no" questions or "more-or-less" questions, and it is clear that rules and standards also entail this kind of simple choice in decision-making. Where a problem consists of several interrelated factors, the adversarial process of the law court and the right-or-wrong application of the rule does not work satisfactorily.

The purpose of discussing Jowell's work at length is to emphasize the importance of deciding whether in fact a particular kind of discretionary action can be subject to either legalization or judicialization. In town planning, there must be doubt whether the multifaceted problems of land-use allocation and control can reasonably be subject to rules, both because they *are* multifaceted and because there can be no certainty that a problem will recur, or worse, can even be foreseen.

The potential judicialization of planning poses rather different questions. The success in Britain of the quasi-judicial public inquiry suggests that judicialization is both possible and desirable, but the limitations of the adversarial approach have been criticized in major public inquiries and the move away from the judicial model would appear to have accelerated since the 1970s. The emphasis on pre-inquiry meetings and the introduction of informal hearings all tend in the direction of greater accessibility and participation in the process (House of Commons 1986) and perhaps also the representation of multiple viewpoints. There is also the question of the basis used for adjudication. On the one hand, there is the point already raised about whether the possibility of recourse to judicial determination allows substantive rights, as well as merely procedural ones (Jowell 1973, Adler & Asquith 1981). On the other, adjudication based on legal rules must tend, we can argue, to encourage a legalistic approach, which will be concerned about whether the rule has been complied with rather than with the justification for the rule in the first place. Legalization of planning thus runs the risk of failing to cope with the complexity of planning problems, limits true participation in the decision-making process, and fails to explore fully the justification for decisions taken.

Britain: discretion accorded by law

Britain, with its emphasis on flexibility has, as we have seen, offered its local authorities wide discretion in the control of development and in the first instance this is clearly a case of high-order agency discretion. This is not some kind of high-minded altruism on the part of central government. In part, it has to do with Lagroye & Wright's "residual domain" theory, in that central government has accepted long since that town planning was something in which it did not wish to be directly involved (although we noted that there was some argument on this score in the 1940s). Planning represented one of those activities that city fathers saw as an appropriate part of civic responsibility. Thus, discretion to act was also seen as important in promoting development, and the flexibility was part of the pro-development stance of the inter-war years. Ward (1974) has suggested that the planning and housing legislation of the 1920s and 1930s was an attempt to show that social democracy in a mixed economy would provide quite as well for its people as could fascism or communism. To some extent this was reinforced by the nationalization of development rights after the war. The state did indeed take development rights unto itself, but it always insisted, albeit with greater or lesser fervour according to the political complexion of the government in power, that there was a policy presumption in favour of development (Grant 1992). Local authorities must be allowed to act flexibly to that end.

Within the Town and Country Planning Acts, local authorities are in principle left entirely free to determine the material considerations that are relevant to a particular planning application, and the same section of the Act allows them to impose such conditions on planning permission "as they think fit" (§70). This is clearly not the end of the story, however. First, this apparently free-ranging dis-cretionary power is subject to a series of important constraints. Secondly, several different discretions play their part in British development control. The primary discretion offered by the acts is to the local planning authority as an agency. This is very largely political discretion, which rests with the authority as a corporate body of elected representatives answerable to their electorate. But important forms of officer discretion also operate in British development control. In par-ticular, the professional discretion of officers, rooted in understanding of pro-fessional expertise, which is jealously guarded by the Royal Town Planning Institute, is at least as important as the political discretion of members.

Limitations to discretionary power

The effective limitations on discretionary power are essentially twofold. The first is through the action of the courts. Since 1947, in successive cases, judges have been at pains to define what might or might not be material to planning applica-tions. The determination of reasons for this elaboration go back to the general discussion above of discretion in relation to administrative law. The fact that the

1947 Act nationalized development rights inevitably led to a concerted attempt to ensure that discretionary power in the Act had as little impact on private property rights as possible. McAuslan (1980) has characterized this process of attrition by the courts as a clash of ideologies: private property rights at war with public interest law.

Successive judgements tried to establish the frontiers of discretionary power beyond which local authorities would be acting *ultra vires*, but even with these frontiers there might be exceptions. Thus, the personal circumstances of the applicant were not usually material, nor, too, was the financial liability of the end–user. All of this jurisprudence has been distilled by central government in the first of its Planning Policy Guidance Notes (PPGs), in the words, which for all they appear bewilderingly circular, are drawn directly from a judgment:

> The "other material considerations" . . . can cover a wide field: "In principle any consideration which relates to the use of land is capable of being a planning consideration" . . . [They] must, however, be genuine planning consideration, i.e. they must be related to the purpose of planning legislation, which is to regulate the development and use of land. (DOE 1988: para. 20)

Much the same has happened with the discretion to impose conditions. On several occasions, the courts have attempted to set parameters within which that discretion may be exercised. This emerged in this final form in the six-point test that has been incorporated into government advice to local authorities since 1968. The points are as follows: the necessity for the condition, its relationship to planning, its relationship to the development for which permission has been granted, its enforceability, its precision, and its reasonableness (DOE 1985). The power to impose conditions that is offered by the Act is substantially constrained by this test.

Yet in spite of this kind of limitation, local planning authorities still retain a wide margin for manoeuvre, which may be upheld by the courts themselves. The case of the extension to the Royal Opera House in Covent Garden is, in this respect, classic. In order to finance a major extension, the Opera House proposed to include offices as part of its development proposal, even though further office development was not countenanced by the local plan. Westminster City Council, the local planning authority, nevertheless granted the Opera House planning permission. The local residents' and traders' groups were, however, enraged by the decision, which they said flew in the face of policy in the local plan to maintain local businesses and residential accommodation. The case was taken to law, and the judge upheld Westminster's case, that the maintenance of the Opera House was also an objective of the local plan, that the extension was necessary to ensure its survival by providing modern backstage facilities and that the offices were essential to the funding of the scheme (Grant 1992). The local authority had used its discretion to depart from one aspect of its committed policy to support another, and the reason, although not apparently admissible as "material", could nevertheless be justified by reference to local land-use policy.

Decisions by the courts are not, however, the only means by which the discretionary power of local authorities is kept in check. At least as important is the role of national policy directives in Circulars and Policy Guidance Notes. We saw how already in the 1920s, Parliament was enacting legislation that gave local authorities leeway to act flexibly, but how central government could not refrain from advising them to act with restraint. We have also noted how government Circulars have a central role in appeals against local authority refusals of permission. In the end what is at issue here is a tussle between two discretions: that of central government to direct national policy for land-use and development and that of local authorities to determine their own specific criteria for what is material. The way in which central policy in Circulars and local policy interact, whether implied in a decision or explicit in a plan, is an example of the general interaction between the two levels of government that Rhodes refers to. Within the specific domain of planning control, local authorities are neither as free as they appear to be, given the wording of the Act (nor for that matter as they might wish to be), but they are by no means entirely under the thumb of central government directives.

Planning agreements and obligations

Another important area of discretion is the power that local authorities have to enter into agreements with intending developers. This power is of a different order to the others. Whereas other development control decisions imply that the role of the local authority is that of impartial arbiter acting for the public good, the ability to enter agreements is based upon an understanding of a negotiated mutual benefit. The local planning authority is implicated in the use of agreements in a way that as a controlling authority it is theoretically not. We saw in Chapter 2 how freeing the power to make agreements from the need for ministerial approval was seen as a way of increasing the flexibility and responsiveness of the planning system to the need for development. Yet planning agreements have proved to be an awkward genie once let out of the bottle.

The difficulty with this kind of discretionary power is that, unlike the freedom to impose conditions and determine material considerations, it is inherently not susceptible to external control. An agreement is a private contract between two organizations, that in theory at least must be mutually agreed to exist at all. When developers complained that local planning authorities were exercising undue leverage on them to secure benefits, there was practically very little that the government could do. Part of the problem was defining what the limits of agreements should properly be. The DOE's Property Advisory Group deliberated on the matter (1982) and their advice was incorporated in a Circular (DOE 1983). But the Circular did not clarify the proper use of agreements, and the problem for government was that it could not ensure that its advice was heeded in this instance through the appeals procedure.

119

More recent evidence suggests that the use of agreements has not in any case been abusive, in spite of the anecdotes that have circulated (Grimley J. R. Eve 1992). The government did in the end find a way to bring the use of agreements rather more closely under its control by the introduction of planning obligations in the Planning and Compensation Act. This not only allowed developers to make unilateral declarations of intent on the infrastructure they might provide to supplement their projects, but required that these were to be considered as material considerations. This was a curious thing to do, because, where the government had once suspected local authorities of either of extorting benefits or selling planning permissions, it was now positively encouraging developers to buy planning permissions.

Problems with discretionary planning

Flexibility is the essential characteristic of the British system, even if it is held in check by a variety of mechanisms. For many commentators, this discretionary power is the great strength of British development control. Yet there is no question that it is also the source of confusion and incoherence. The question of the control of architectural design is perhaps the most telling general example of the difficulties that allowing material considerations to be defined by policy and practice can run into. In the wording of the development control sections of the Town and Country Planning Act 1947 and its successors, there is little explicit reference to aesthetics, design or external appearance as material to decisions on planning applications. On the other hand, from the outset, legal opinion appears to have held that matters of aesthetics were a fit consideration in development control.

However, this control was exercised in the absence of any clearly defined policies, at either national or local level (Punter 1986, 1987, Booth 1987). Central government opinion has fluctuated considerably in a tradition that pre-dates the 1947 Act. In the 1950s much of the effort on design advice was put into layout design and architectural detailing for public housing. In the 1960s, the introduction of Conservation Areas – areas of special architectural interest, the character and appearance of which it is desirable to preserve and enhance (Town and Country Planning (Conservation and Listed Buildings) Act 1990: §69) – led to an enthusiasm for tighter aesthetic control. From this came the landmark in local authority policy in the Essex *Design guide for residential areas* (Essex County Council 1973), but the attacks on what were seen as delaying tactics by local authorities were specifically targeted at the problems created by design control. This in turn led central government in the 1980s to stress the importance of allowing developers freedom to exercise their design capabilities, and limiting involvement by local authorities (DOE 1980). At the same time others have called for simple rules that would set the limits to what was seen as local authority interference. In 1992, the Royal Institute of British Architects and Royal Town Planning Institute seem to have reached agreement by establishing ten principles of design control that the government included in an appendix to its revised PPG1 (DoE 1992). Yet in 1995, the Royal Institute of British Architects has again called for "clear and measurable guidelines" that would circumvent "the aesthetic whims of councillors and planning officials" (*Planning Week* 1995). In this case, flexibility and discretion, so far from sharpening the responsiveness of the development control system, has simply led to unresolved conflict.

Discretionary power in practice

At the local level the interplay of these various discretionary freedoms is best seen through case studies. With conditions, local authorities have long been in the practice of establishing lists of standard conditions that can be used in the development control process. The reason for this is in part attributable to the pitfalls that the unwary may fall into if a decision is ever contested in the courts. But the use of standard conditions does also seem to fall into the general feature of administrative practice described by Noble (1981), in that, faced with completely open-ended discretion, administrators like to find rules to guide their decision-making. Underwood (1980: 159) puts it succinctly:

> Most caseworkers would defend the scope here for the exercise of discretion in the formulation of recommendations from the basis of professional expertise and judgement. In practice, however, as has been shown, the organizational and institutional pressures on the caseworker tend to lead to attempts to regulate the development control task to one where it is possible to work in accordance with rules. This brings a much needed sense of security to a job that is full of uncertainties and the stress of conflicting demands.

Lists of standard conditions are only one of the means whereby development control officers regulate the tensions that discretionary freedom brings.

On the other hand, there is some evidence from case studies in Yorkshire and Derbyshire that local planning authorities have in fact not necessarily used conditions in a way that respects the parameters imposed by government advice. Conditions used to promote the quality of design could all too often be imprecise and unenforceable, even when they were necessary (Booth 1983). The fact that the local authorities got away with this use of discretion was because the conditions were not onerous enough to warrant an appeal. But there was real doubt as to whether they served any useful purpose, other than as a means of trying to affirm the local authorities' control.

There are plenty of examples to show how the more general discretion to determine the material considerations is used. The Tesco case at Meadowhead, Sheffield, shows a variety of different discretions at work. It shows how the balance of considerations may be finely weighted and the correct solution far from obvious. The scheme as originally presented was, in the judgement of the planning officers, too much development for the size of the site and its access. They, therefore, proceeded to negotiate with the developer to achieve a scaled-down version of the project before it was submitted for formal planning approval. Concurrently, they negotiated three agreements that would have been put into effect if permission had been granted. The first was on the provision of alternative playing fields, on a site that, as we noted, was on the green belt and straddled the city's boundary with North East Derbyshire District. The second was on the provision of open space to be dedicated to public use on completion. The third was on improvement to the main roads to accommodate traffic entering and leaving the site. The package together was sufficient to persuade officers that the scheme could now be recommended to the planning committee for approval. Councillors, however, were by now well aware of the upsurge of public opinion against the scheme and, in the event, refused planning permission in spite of their officers' recommendations. This decision was of course later upheld at the public inquiry into the appeal.

In this case the City Council as a whole, that is to say officers and elected representatives together, were acting correctly within the framework provided by the law. They were perfectly entitled to exercise the discretion either in favour or against the Tesco scheme, provided they could justify the decision. Agency discretion was therefore part and parcel of this decision, as in any decision in a planning application. But the outcome of the case also rested on the professional judgement of officers, the kind of discretion that required a sophisticated interpretation of policy. It was not a question of applying rules, because there were none; but there were general policies about open spaces that applied to cases more or less like this, and a general principle, that of "over-development", never fully defined, whose interpretation was entirely dependent on the esoteric knowledge of the professional officers.

The discretion of committee members to refuse the application depended on a different rationale. Their main concern was for the opinion of their electorate, which meant that residents' interests were far more heavily weighted in the final decision than were the developers. Although the developers could then criticize the decision as political, they were in fact using the same source of basic data but valued in a different way, such that "residents' amenity" became the overriding factor. In some ways, this value system was rather more transparent than that of the officers' professional judgement. The point becomes clear when we note that the officers who were able to defend the committee decision on appeal without apparent qualms: in the event the "political" decision could be easily assimilated to professional judgement.

Another case shows the way in which the discretion available in the Act can be used to approve development. The case concerns competing proposals for two superstores in the outskirts of Plymouth. Here the City Council were prepared to sanction a departure from the local plans for one superstore near to an important road intersection. Sainsbury and Tesco both expressed interest in the site, and the city council invited them to compete for it on the basis of a package of fringe benefits offered as a planning obligation. Both companies agreed to the

122

competition and Tesco won the site with a range of benefits that included a crèche and a children's play area. The case came to the courts when a third retailer, the Co-op, called for a judicial review of the decision. They had an interest in a site that in the local plan was allocated for retail development in a nearby district centre and they were concerned that the market was not large enough for two superstores. However, the argument on which the call for a judicial review was based was that the city council had acted beyond its powers in determining the decision on the fringe benefits contained in an obligation under the Planning Acts. The judge nevertheless ruled that, for the council to act as it did, was perfectly acceptable given that planning obligations were defined by law as material considerations (Ashworth 1993, Gilbert 1993). The case appeared to confirm the worst fears of those who saw developers buying planning permission under the change in the law, but even more recent case law has suggested that in legal terms the Plymouth case is not the last word (Brock 1994). Leaving aside the planning obligations, however, the case demonstrates how much freedom local authorities have to depart from the policies and the plans they themselves have prepared.

France: the control of discretion

The French planning system, dedicated to certainty, has no such confidence in dealing with flexibility and discretion, largely because these are seen as a threat to the certainty that the system is designed to deliver. In coming to the French system, I was convinced in an Englishly pragmatic way, that it could not function as the books described because there would always be unforeseen circumstances that required a flexible response. In that I was proved right, but the interest lay not in the fact that there was discretion available in the French system, but how it was made available and what the consequences of its use were. As with the British system, discretion is present by virtue of powers conferred, the legislation, professional judgement, political will and administrative convenience.

Types of agency discretion

The first issue with France is to enquire how far local authorities as agencies really did acquire discretion to act under the decentralization statutes from 1982 onwards. In some ways the concept of the *état de droit*, coupled to a centralized administration seen as necessary to maintain the unity of the state, have made the question of local–central relations a little more difficult than is the case in Britain. The transfer of planning powers in 1983 demonstrates the point. In principle the Loi Defferre confirmed the right of the commune to administer itself freely without hierarchical control. To the commune was then given the right to initiate plan-making and, once the plan had been in force for six months, the right to determine applications for *permis de construire* in the name of the commune.

123

Thus, the discretion to act in development control was firmly tied to the approval of detailed and specific regulations in the *POS*: if mayors were to be given new powers, then they must be firmly tied to the rule of law. Moreover, although communes were to be free to choose the technical services that prepared the *POS*, the state was nevertheless by law involved in the working group that remained responsible for the preparation of the plan. And the prefect was given a right to modify the *POS* if there no *SD* in force for the area.

There were two further limits to the transfer of powers in 1983. One was the *règle de constructibilité limitée*, which limited new development to the existing built-up areas of communes without a *POS*. At least part of the reason for this regulation was to ensure that the country was properly covered by rules for new development that would not leave decisions open to discretionary whim. The other was the fact that the *DDE* were put at the disposal of communes, free of charge in the exercise of their new responsibilities. This was both a generous recognition by central government of the difficulties that faced small communes in the exercise of their new responsibilities and a way of ensuring that communes did not stray too far out of line by keeping them under the eye of the technical services of the state. The conclusion that many commentators came to at the time was that decentralization offered little in the way of increased power to the communes (Wilson 1988).

Nevertheless, if there was not the kind of global agency discretion in development control decision-making that is accorded by the British Town and Country Planning Acts to British local authorities, there were ways in which the regulatory framework could be made to offer discretionary power. The most potent was through the *NA* zoning for land allocated for future development, subject to the provision of the necessary infrastructure. Through the negotiations that became an inevitable part of the decision on what infrastructure was required, a mayor could secure useful gains for the commune. Thus, in the case of the housing development at Le Long des Feuillis at St-Priest, the mayor was not merely able to get the developer to cede part of the land for social housing, but also to insist that the land was at the front of the site. At Le Soleil Levant in Vernaison, where again *NA* land was involved, part of the discussion on infrastructure involved a road widening that the *communauté urbaine* had not programmed but which was deemed necessary if the housing was to go ahead. The *NA* zoning carries with it an implied agency discretion that communes and intercommunal syndicates are evidently happy to use in pursuit of their own objectives.

The second kind of agency discretion is offered by the *Code de l'urbanisme* itself, in the *RNU*. This part of the code is striking for the extent to which individual rules offer an option to the decision-maker. No fewer than 17 of the 32 articles offer such freedom, and 10 of these articles allow conditions to be imposed. The typical wording of such clauses reads: "Permission may be refused or granted only subject to special conditions"; the key change here lies in the substitution of the word "may" (*peut*) for the word "must" (*doit*) (Jégouzo & Pittard 1981). This may not be agency discretion on the scale of that offered by

British planning law, but nevertheless is extensive and begins to give the lie to the idea that a rule-based system precludes discretionary freedom and flexibility.

The third kind of discretion is that offered by the regulations of the *POS*, which represents an interesting example of an agency offering itself discretion, since the makers of the regulations are likely to be those who have a say in applying them. A good example would be the zoning *URM* used in the *POS* for Lyon, devised to allow for the complexity of land use and the physical form of development in the inner urban areas. The rubric to the regulation reads:

> The issue here is to break with the systematic use of block layout regulations, in favour of a more flexible prescriptive system relying largely on detailed drawn limits. (Agence d'Urbanisme de la Communauté Urbaine de Lyon 1985)

In practice these regulations appear to leave considerable leeway for developers, and for decision-makers to exercise their judgement in determining cases at the point at which an application is made.

The important point about all these kinds of agency discretion has to do with the agency upon whom the discretion is conferred. Overwhelmingly in France, the discretionary power is administrative and not political and is exercised by the administration at all its levels. There is no concept of the power to decide being vested in an authority of elected representatives, and the administration forms, in theory at least, a continuum from President of the Republic to the mayor of the commune. A particularly strong beneficiary of this power is the *DDE*, called to act on behalf of the state and all too frequently for communes in the exercise of their decentralized powers. With the *RNU*, for example, it is the *DDE* who are the beneficiaries of the discretionary power, for it is they who in most cases take decisions on applications for *permis de construire* in communes without a *POS* in force. But in the other examples, the technical services on which discretion is conferred are local and not national. In the wording of the *POS* for Lyon, for example, the technical services appear to be formalizing the desire and need for flexibility and consolidating their hold over the decision-making process. With *NA* zoning, the discretion is not formalized but only implied; once again the technical services have a large stake in the power that may be exercised.

At the local level the mayor of the commune does, however, also become a discretionary actor, in that, where a *POS* is in force, it is he or she who determines the application in the name of the commune. In that sense, decentralization of powers in 1983 has meant a real increase in discretionary power that becomes potentially more political than technical. The limitation of resources means, however, that technical services of one kind or another still exercise a large measure of command, whether the agency is national or local. Mayors also appear to be able to influence decisions to release *NA* land, even if, there too, the technical services may be heavily implicated. The interesting question is how far mayors are in fact able to influence the course of events, given the very heavy pressure of technicians at one remove from direct control.

125

The simple answer appears to be that mayors can exercise considerable tactical leverage in the process to achieve a desired outcome. At Le Soleil Levant, the change from the *NC* to an *NA* zoning was the will of the mayor, as it was also in the conditions that were imposed on the release of land for the St-Priest estate of Le Long des Feuillis. The most obvious case of all was in the decision on the extension to the depot of Transports Griset at Vernaison. In Chapter 5 we remarked on the way in which certainties had been eroded by the choice offered in the regulations by the *POS* to permit extensions to existing commercial and industrial development. Here a general assumption in favour of allowing the extension to proceed coincided with a strong desire on the part of the mayor to grant permission and thus ensure that a major source of employment and tax was not lost to the commune.

Why are mayors in cases such as these able to get the decision they want? The particular circumstances of each case offers a partial explanation, but underlying the particularities is the general status accorded to communes and their mayors in the political economy of the country. Provided a mayoral decision can be justified in law, technical services will not wish to oppose the mayor on the grounds of appropriateness. Moreover, the ancient respect for local democracy represented by the commune is now bolstered by the knowledge that in many cases the *DDE* is no longer entirely indispensable to the commune. Since decentralization, mayors are not obliged to turn to the *DDE* for technical support, even if most do. The discretionary power of mayors stems ultimately from the role they are perceived as playing in the French state.

Officer discretion: applying and departing from rules

As significant as the discretion offered to agencies through the wording of the regulations is the officers' discretion in the interpretation of regulations as they are made to apply to given cases. Here again Le Soleil Levant exemplifies the discretionary behaviour of both technical services and elected representatives. The underlying assumption was that development should go ahead, perhaps, we might add, because the mayor wanted it. The process of negotiation was therefore devoted as much as anything else to finding an interpretation of the rules that would both satisfy the need for legality and ensure that development could take place. In this, the technical services acted as facilitators rather than controllers, making themselves indispensable to the mayor and to developers alike. The case of the cul-de-sac at Le Long des Feuillis is even more striking in this respect. The technical services specifically sought ways of overcoming the restriction in road length that they themselves had been instrumental in defining.

The problem with exercising discretionary power in this way is that it is essentially covert. There is no clear indication when the rules will be interpreted in a given way and what criteria will be used. Charges of expediency and even corruption thus become all too easy to make, even if all too difficult to prove. However, there is a double game observable in this discussion of the French case studies. Mayors were seeking to circumvent rules in order to favour their own projects and thus to retain a degree of control over outcomes, even if that control was tactical. The administrators who collude with them are also able to display their control over the system. As guardians of the rules, administrators are in the privileged position of knowing how to mould them to the needs of their clients, mayors or developers alike. In doing so the role of the technical and administrative power is enhanced and officer discretion becomes a question of managing relationships as well as influencing a course of events (see Dupuy & Thoenig 1985).

Flexibility in US and Hong Kong zoning plans

We saw in Chapter 4 how, in the USA, the rigidity of zoning ordinances was circumvented in part by zoning techniques and in part by the use of variances. The striking point was that commentators both recognize the need for this flexibility and fear its consequences. From within, Rose (1969) saw four preconditions as essential to the effective operation of rigid zoning. Babcock (1966: 12) inveighs against the confusion that discretionary techniques of one kind or another have created and suggest that it is the product not of "uncontrolled individual enterprise" on the US model but "a combination of controls and lack of controls, of over-planning and anti-planning, enterprise and anti-enterprise, all in absolute disarray". Cullingworth, as an external observer 27 years on, emphasizes this complexity in very much the same way as Rose.

Variances

Both the power to issue variances and the range of zoning techniques discussed below are agency discretion in that both are expressly provided for by legally sanctioned documents. But they are nevertheless of a rather different order. Variances are made possible by the Standard State Enabling Act itself that:

> confers on the board of adjustment the power "to authorize upon appeal in specific cases such variance from the terms of the ordinance as well not be contrary to the public interest, where, owing to special conditions, a literal enforcement of the provisions of the ordinance will result in unnecessary hardship, and so that the spirit of the ordinance shall be observed and substantial justice done." (Cullingworth 1993: 46)

So, with variances, the discretionary agency is the Board of Adjustment, which is given general criteria within the Act by which it must exercise that discretion. Inevitably too, the generalized criteria of the act have become refined by jurisprudence. In the judgments that the Boards of Adjustment take, Cullingworth makes it clear that they are not simply the creatures of the municipality and "commonly operate according to their own sense of what is right, with little regard for the law or even their local planning department" (ibid.: 47). This is a classic form of agency discretion akin to that offered by the British legislation, in which the legislature confers a wide-ranging power on the Boards of Adjustment.

Zoning techniques

The power to use zoning techniques to introduce flexibility into zoning is essentially similar to the way in which the POS may contain discretionary clauses. This is not officer discretion in Bull's terms, because the regulations make clear the nature of discretion available to the decision-maker. But, as with the POS, the power is conferred by the planning commission on itself: the roles of legislator and executor are combined. However, it is worth looking at the techniques themselves in a little more detail, because there are variations in the degree of open-endedness that they imply, and indeed in who the main beneficiaries of a discretion are. They vary, too, in the extent to which they are regarded as legitimate. Five such devices are commonly listed (see Rose 1969, Wakeford 1990, Cullingworth 1993).

The most obviously contentious technique, and the one that is most obviously open to abuse, is spot zoning. This refers to the practice of modifying the zoning ordinance for a given site. Here, the courts have sniffed out all too frequently a favouritism on the part of the local planning commissions that looks potentially corrupt. Equally, it might have its uses in relieving the sterility of single-use zones. The fundamental trouble is that spot zoning flies in the face of the concept of one law applying to all: it denies the comprehensiveness of the zoning ordinance and plan (if there is one) on which it is based, and incites neighbours to apply for upgrading.

The second technique, floating zoning, is the means by which a planning commission may establish regulations for a kind of development that it seeks, without specifying the location to which it applies. The location is fixed when the developer comes forward with a proposal for a given area. Wakeford (1990: 64) considers that they "are perhaps a political cop-out" and certainly they appear to be an abdication of responsibility for the distribution of activities that from a British perspective would be an essential part on the planning process. To that extent, floating zones offer an important discretionary freedom to the developers. Cullingworth notes that they are also used where low-cost higher-density housing is looked for in a low-density area. In such circumstances the floating zoning ensures that land prices are not pushed up and the objective of the zoning is not thereby lost.

A third technique is the planned unit development that, within a given area, allows for a wide range of uses, without the form of the development being identified in the ordinance. The zoning ordinance does not, therefore, specify the full range of constraints, but may identify performance criteria that developers are supposed to meet. The effect is to offer some considerable freedom to developers to produce a proposal that "on approval . . . is effectively bound into the ordinance" (Wakeford 1990: 65). On the other hand, as Cullingworth (1993: 54) explains:

> This approach necessitates negotiations between the developer and the municipality: this is the mechanism by which flexibility is achieved. This is a far cry from zoning.

A fourth technique is that of the special district, which is used to protect the particular use character of a given area and where "the intention is to shield the area from market forces" (Cullingworth 1993: 58). These special district zonings overlay the generic zonings of major urban areas and appear to have found favour particularly in San Francisco, with no fewer than 16 such districts. Wakeford writes with some admiration of the device and reflects on whether it might not be a useful tool in British planning control. Cullingworth is less complimentary. Although he accepts that it is not necessarily wrong for planning authorities to try and counter market forces, he sees special districts as being a largely ineffectual response to local political pressure. The major weakness of the special district for him, however, is that the decision, to create such a district is not taken in relation to an overall planning framework.

The fifth technique is of a different order. Incentive zoning, or zoning bonuses, allow developers to secure an increase in zoning allowances in exchange for providing a public benefit of some kind. An early example was the possibility offered to developers in Manhattan to provide a plaza in exchange for an increased floor area ratio, although as Wakeford notes the 1961 New York ordinance introduced the plaza incentive as a sweetener for the general reduction in development rights that the new ordinance had introduced. The point about this incentive was that it did not *require* developers to provide a plaza, merely that, should they do so, they might benefit from the increased development right. Since the value of the increased floorspace was very considerably greater than the cost of providing the plaza, it is scarcely surprising that developers in the main did choose to do so. The idea of incentive zoning caught on, and the practice extended to different kinds of incentive in cities across the USA. There is no question but that incentive zoning has been successful in securing the immediate end – in the case of Manhattan – public open space in the form of plazas. But, as Cullingworth notes, the wisdom of using incentive zoning is doubtful and the cost great; the utility of many plazas in downtown Manhattan is not entirely evident. It moved zoning away from a simple establishment of development rights to a procedure in which both developer and public authority stand to gain, to the detriment of long-term planning policy.

These techniques differ in the extent to which they make clear the basis on which decisions are taken. Spot zoning is inevitably problematic, because the decision must by its nature be *ad hoc* and the validity of a decision is not therefore accessible from outside. Floating and special district zoning at least establish at the outset what criteria are being used, even if the firstmay be a cop-out and the second a response to political whim. The planned unit development, although dependent on negotiation that may not be easily accessible, at least produces an agreement that effectively binds the developer. Incentive zoning, too, is on the face of it an open procedure because the incentives and the public benefits are identified in the ordinance itself. The problem here is the way in which the cumulative impact of bonusing may undermine effective planning. All these practices have become necessary to overcome what is seen as the straitjacket of zoning. All of them appear to call into question the very basis on which zoning is built.

Hong Kong

In Hong Kong, as in France and the USA, the development of a system of zoning plans has led simultaneously to a search for flexibility in the way in which those plans are applied to particular developments. We have already noted how the plans divide uses into Column 1 and Column 2, in which the former are permitted as of right but the latter require a planning application. A further discretionary power has been added since the 1991 amendment to the Town Planning Ordinance, which allows the creation of Development Permission Areas "for areas which require immediate planning control prior to the preparation of Outline Zoning Plans, mainly for non-urban areas" (Hong Kong 1991: 17). Development Permission Areas are short-life plans, prepared for a finite period of three years and may not be renewed. But rather as interim development control allowed local authorities in Britain to control development in areas in which they had declared their intention to prepare a plan under the 1932 Town and Country Planning Act, so, too, all developments in Development Permission Areas are likely to need express planning consent. In principle, Development Permission Areas are, however, more than just boundaries on a map, because they may identify zones with Column 1 and Column 2 uses in the same way as Outline Zoning Plans and may also identify uses that are permitted everywhere as of right. Elsewhere only the existing uses are permitted: all other development is subject to the need for planning permission. In practice, Development Permission Area plans do not appear to carry the degree of elaboration that the ordinance allows for. Development is, moreover, defined in a way that is closely modelled on the post-war British legislation, to cover both building operations and material change of use.

These forms of flexibility all entail agency discretion: the powers are conferred by law and in effect on the Town Planning Board. The difficulty they are designed to address, however, is of a rather different order to that we have observed in France or in the USA. What appears to be happening is an attempt to disentangle the relationship between rights to land use, conferred by lease agreements, from the right to future development, which leases also conferred on the lessee. This desire to establish discretionary power takes place under two particular conditions. The first we have already noted: the Hong Kong government is not a neutral observer in the process, because of the large contribution that development makes to government revenue. Maintaining a climate of certainty for developers is thus seen as essential to Hong Kong's prosperity. The second is that the tradition of administration remains a derivative of British practice, and Britain remains a point of reference for its planners who were in part educated there or in other parts of the English-speaking world. The system of control is partly imbued with a system of discretionary planning and in the trust of the administration that agency discretion implies. Hong Kong exhibits a particular kind of tension between certainty and flexibility, which throws a new light both on the relationship between landownership and planning control and the differences between regulatory and discretionary planning.

Discretion: some conclusions

One kind of conclusion to draw from the examples explored above would be about the merits of discretionary as against regulatory planning, and to argue, as Wakeford does in relation to the USA, that discretionary systems are drawn towards a greater regulation in a quest for certainty and that regulatory systems inevitably seek ways around the inherent rigidity by a series of devices. However, this kind of antithesis does not reflect the discussion on the nature of discretion with which this chapter began. What is needed is an analysis of the types of discretion available and how they are used in practice. The key questions are Dworkin's: the standards or authority to which the discretionary power must refer.

The agency discretion offered by British legislation is set within very wide limits indeed. At the same time it is subject to a series of limitations, even if, as we noted, it can be used with a wide degree of imagination in practice. One kind of constraint is that offered by central government in its Circulars and planning advice, which from the 1920s were a call to order by offering criteria and standards to which local authorities, as beneficiaries of discretionary power, were expected to conform. The other form of constraint was that imposed by case law, which, although relatively limited, has defined the parameters of discretion in several important areas. The constraints are, therefore, largely external to the controlling authorities. The planning systems of France, the USA and Hong Kong, for all that they are essentially regulatory and not discretionary in character, nevertheless offer certain kinds of limited agency discretion, which are of some significance. France offers discretion in the clauses of the *RNU*; the USA in its Standard Enabling Act allows for variances to the zoning ordinances in force. But much of this discretion is in fact the discretionary agency articulating the limits of its own power to act, or indeed widening those limits. Hence, there are the regulations in *POS* that reflect the complexity of urban areas; there are the

131

Column 2 uses that may be permitted in Hong Kong's Outline Zoning Plans; and there is the clutch of devices in US zoning ordinances that change zoning from fixed limits to negotiated agreements.

Officer discretion is equally apparent, at any rate in France and Britain. The regulatory nature of French planning appears to invite discretionary behaviour on the part of officers, of various kinds. We observed a process whereby rules were seen as constraints to be circumvented in the interests of allowing development to proceed; there was debate about how rules were to be applied and whether they could be broken. In Britain the cases suggest that it is important to distinguish between the agency discretion conferred on the local planning authority, formed of elected representatives, and the behaviour of individual officers dealing with planning applications and advising the decision-making committee. The Tesco case, for example, revealed this distinction well. The interesting point is to know what standards officers refer to in exercising this discretion. As Underwood (1980) has argued, much of the decision-making of officers in British local authorities relates to an implicit set of values that form the ethos of the planning profession. French decision-makers clearly refer to a very different set of standards that appear rooted in a view of administrative ethics, rather than professional values. The discretionary actor is not a guardian of policy so much as an enabler, an *interlocuteur privilégié* to help the *administré* through the complexities of law, regulation and procedure. For both, however, discretion is intimately bound up with the desire to maintain status and credibility.

Discussion of the use of discretionary planning thus affects two separate if interconnected issues. On the one hand, there are the ends to which discretionary power is put, and the case studies looked at the way in which discretion has been used to achieve certain kinds of objectives. On the other hand, discretion is about process, about who decides and with what degrees of freedom, about the way in which the system legitimates the power to act. The question that arises sooner or later whenever discretion is discussed is this: how are those who assume discretionary powers called to account for what they do?

CHAPTER 7
Accountability

Much of the discussion about discretion and the power to take decisions hovered around the parameters within which the decision was taken. The problem of the criteria used to evaluate the decision, and the extent to which a decision could be tested, surfaces in all the case studies. The clarity of the criteria and their derivation were all from time to time at issue. But in addition to the parameters set for the decision there is also a question of the process and the procedures that ensure accountability. And if those with power are called to account for what they do, who in turn decides the standards by which they are judged? One of the difficulties in dealing with discretionary power is that one set of discretions can all too often be overlaid by another, or as Ham & Hill (1984: 160) put it in relation to forms of judicial accountability:

> to counteract the discretionary behaviour of officials with the rule of law merely comes up against a further set of discretionary actors, the judges.

Another problem is that the criteria that are used in reaching decisions interlock with the mechanisms put in place to ensure the accountability of those decisions. These are some of the issues that this chapter deals with.

Forms of accountability

In all the systems that have been considered, different forms of accountability operate to ensure that decisions are indeed accounted for. In that all are linked to a democratic form of government, there is one kind of accountability through the ballot box. British local authorities have discretionary power conferred upon them by the Town and Country Planning Acts, and as elected representatives they answer to their electorate for the political powers they possess. Councils employ officials to administer the activities in the local authorities' power and the officials are directly accountable for what they do to the councillors who employ them. So, too, at central government level, ministers are answerable to Parliament for the activities of their ministries. These electoral relationships hold more or less good for all the systems of development control touched on in this book.

Much the same goes for the accountability before the law that all actors in controlling development are subject to, for all that there are wide differences in the legal system. Finally, all the systems have some forms of administrative accountability, which are effectively a kind of hierarchical control by one layer of administration over another. These systems are intended to complement each other.

In practice, there are snags that render all these forms of responsibility less than effective in preventing abuses of power. The electoral process may be good for holding politicians to account for the cumulative effect of decisions that they take, but it is rare for local politicians to be voted out of office for a single development control decision. Only the most gross cases of misconduct lead to resignation. Then the link between electorate, politicians and administrators may be so attenuated that there is no effective accountability at all. In the 1950s, the scandal of Crichel Down, a case concerning the return of land used by the Ministry of Defence during the Second World War, exposed, in the words of Harlow & Rawlings (1984: 43), "a world of administrative policy and decision-making apparently immune from political and parliamentary control". Finally, professionals in both local and central government will consider themselves to have a responsibility to written and unwritten codes of conduct, whose purpose is in part to maintain the status of their profession, perhaps in the face of political pressure. Although professional accountability may act to counterbalance political discretion, there is no guarantee that it will do so. The possibilities for collusion and arbitrariness remain.

It is against this background that demands for the return of the rule of law are sometimes made, as the means whereby discretionary power may be held in check. Reduce discretion, the argument goes, and make individual actors accountable before the courts. There are two problems with this approach. The first is that it assumes that all decisions may be evaluated in terms of legality or illegality. We have already queried whether legal rules are necessarily the way in which certainty can be assured in the process of controlling development; they now also appear limited in the way in which they can ensure accountability. The second is that it assumes that judicial process is the best means of resolving problems and guaranteeing equity.

In practice, therefore, all systems of development control rely on a variety of methods of ensuring that decision-makers are accountable. But, clearly, different systems give different weight to different forms of accountability. What is important is to discover how effective the accountability is in practice, and the problems brought by the forms of accountability relied upon.

Accountability in regulatory systems

In the regulatory systems of continental Europe, the assumption is that the accountability of the decision-maker is above all to the law, not merely in a general sense but in the detail of the decision that he or she takes. In France, this results in the system of administrative courts, which are designed to make the decision-makers accountable and to offer citizens the right to make their claims against the administration. Hence, as we have seen, policy is expressed in the form of rules against which decisions can be measured; a decision is either legal or it is not. However, a system like this is itself very quickly put to the test if the rules are not simple and clear cut. It is for this reason that discretionary options pose such a problem for the French. In those clauses of the *RNU* or of *POS*, which offer choice to the decision-maker, the very fact of the choice itself tends to put the decision beyond the reach of the law. At Vernaison in the Transports Griset case, a decision either for or against the extension was potentially legal; what was involved was a matter of policy to be determined by professional judgement.

The problem goes well beyond the limited examples cited in the case studies in this book. In a survey of *DDE* staff in the 1970s for example, Tanguy (1979: 50) found a widespread discontent with the manner in which regulations were drawn up; they were "badly written" and "sometimes impossible to apply". Clearly, any difficulties at administrative level would merely be replicated in the courts, too. The point is put succinctly by Prats et al. (1979: 43–4) quoting Brabant et al.:

> The current unease of the administrative judge arises from the question of the very laxity of the "legality" over which he can exercise control; "If the text authorized a departure in an exceptional case, he exercises in that exceptional case only a minimum of control; he is practically disarmed if the administration is purely and simply without other constraint, authorized to depart from a rule."

In practice, of course, the courts themselves become involved in policy decisions, even if that is not intended to be their function. In particular, the administrative judge is able to decide on the basis of an *erreur manifeste d'appréciation* (manifest error of judgement), which becomes important whenever there is discretion offered by the regulations (Jégouzo & Pittard 1981). But the essential dilemma in all this is that accountability of a rule-based system before the courts is weakened whenever discretionary action is possible.

The accountability of decision-makers to third parties through the courts is also a striking feature of the French system of development control, and is in theory one of the great strengths of administrative law. However, the limited evidence of the French case studies is not very encouraging. In the case of Transports Griset, for example, local residents were effectively defeated by the complexities of the process and were thus unable to register their appeal against the decision to allow the extension to the depot. If they had managed to lodge an appeal, it was far from clear that they would have won their case. Given that the *POS* offered decision-makers discretion as to how to determine the application, there was nothing inherently illegal in the decision they took. Third-party rights are limited, too, to those who can demonstrate that they will be adversely affected by the decision taken. This has the effect of casting objectors in the role of indi-

135

viduals whose private property rights are affected, not as people who might wish to give voice to a wider concern for the environment. Residents of Le Pellet were seen to be involved in a neighbour dispute (which in part they most certainly were) and not in a battle to protect amenity.

Important though the courts are in making the system accountable, and difficult though ensuring accountability may be in the face of changing circumstances, legal redress is not the only way in which mayors must account for the development control decisions they take. Since decentralization, use of prefectoral power to vet all decisions taken by mayors of communes has introduced a form of administrative accountability that has considerable significance. The *contrôle de légalité* is of course once again a way of ensuring that mayors have acted in accordance with the law, and the sanction that is available to the prefect is to refer the decision to the court if satisfaction is not obtained. With *permis de construire* the prefect has a two-month period after a decision notice has been issued, in which he or she may contest the decision. Guidance given to prefects in the exercise of this new power suggested that it is more than just a matter of law, however:

> Two particular preoccupations must guide you in the exercise control over planning documents:
> * to ensure that supra-communal interests of all kinds are taken into account;
> * to preserve the interests of the commune itself by avoiding irregularities which might . . . lead to authorizations for development being marred by illegality. (Ministère de l'Urbanisme, du Logement et des Transports/Ministère de l'Intérieur 1984)

Upholding the law is thus also a matter of policy for central government and the prefects. Legal control is seen as necessary to ensure the survival of the national interest, as well as to protect mayors from themselves.

The way that the *contrôle de légalité* is actually used puts an interesting complexion on the accountability it offers. Perhaps the first point to make is that an enormous number of decisions must be considered each year by prefects. In a report on the first year of operation, for example, 3300000 acts were subject to *contrôle de légalité* and of these 13.5 per cent or approximately 440000 were planning matters, including *permis de construire*. Very few of these decisions were actually referred to the courts, on average 20 per *département*. The report noted that cases were frequently withdrawn, which the authors suggested was "a sign of successful consultation between the representative of the State and the author of the act". The conclusion drawn was that the "*contrôle de légalité* has given rise neither to government by judges nor to the replacement of one tutelage by another" (*Le Moniteur des Travaux Publics* 1985: 63).

The figures in the report suggested that there was wide variation in practice between prefects. Périnet-Marquet's study (1986) points to some of the difficulties that prefects faced. In the *département* of Vienne, 8544 decisions on applications for *permis de construire* were subject to control, with only two members of staff to check them. He concluded that under such circumstances control could scarcely be a general one and many decisions would hardly be looked at. Commenting more generally, Périnet-Marquet took the view that the prefects were often too lenient in their approach: "for many prefects, better an illegality than a fight" (ibid.: 270). The *contrôle de légalité* looks very much as though it is another discretionary power, and the prefect another discretionary actor. The *contrôle de légalité* does, moreover, have an interesting impact on the action of the courts themselves, as Chabanol (1986) notes, for example. Where before decentralization the administrative judge adjudicated between the administration and the public at large, now the judge is required to decide between the different wills of separate parts of the administration. In the past, the prefect dealt with conflicts between the *DDE* and mayors of communes; now that decision has to be referred to the courts:

> In the presence of cases which express two different visions of policy, that of the representatives of the State and that of the decentralized local authority, the administrative judge can only take policy decision. That will be difficult for him, because it is not his role. (ibid.: 284)

Contrôle de légalité thus reinforces the judge's role in taking policy decisions, which is already implied by the concept of *erreur manifeste d'appréciation*. Not only is the prefect a discretionary actor, so too is the administrative judge.

The practice of the *contrôle de légalité* in particular cases bears out these general remarks. At Le Soleil Levant, there were three ways in which the project as proposed by the site developer infringed the regulations. We noted how the local administration attempted to accommodate these infringements. Nevertheless, the prefect gave notice that he would refer the decision of the mayor to the court, unless the decision was annulled. However, the interesting point was that, of three potential illegalities, only two were identified by the prefect: the infringement of the *NC* zone and plots on the *espace boisé classé*. Why he should have failed to comment upon the plot size is a matter for conjecture. Maybe he regarded the infringement as too trivial to bother with. Maybe he regarded the two infringements that related to regulations in the code as having a greater significance than a regulation that was derived only from the *POS*. Maybe the infringement was not even noticed. Whatever the reason may be, two points stand out: one is the extent of the prefect's discretion in the use of *contrôle de légalité*; the other is the way in which it appears to encourage decision-makers to take a risk that an illegal decision will not be noticed.

The Mayor of Vernaison did withdraw the original decision, and a modified proposal was approved immediately thereafter. The question of the *espace boisé classé* was to be dealt with by a modification to the *POS* in which there would be some scrutiny of whether the land was indeed woodland or just scrub as the authorities and developer had maintained. The problem of the infringement of the *NC* land was dealt with by moving the boundary of the zone up by one contour line. The developer and the Mayor of Vernaison were in the end to get the development they wanted. In this case, the *contrôle de légalité* looked less like a guarantee of legal rights and a form of accountability than a kind of lottery in which the outcome was derived from an essentially covert process.

The USA also demonstrates the doubling of legal redress with a form of administrative accountability through the use of the Boards of Adjustment. Here the fundamental operating principle is that of the separation of powers: a planning commission that prepares a zoning ordinance cannot be allowed to be responsible for dealing with variances or appeals against zoning imposed. But, as Cullingworth (1993) points out, the separation merely seems to multiply the number of discretionary actors. The Board of Adjustment may not be subject to the same pressures as a municipal planning commission, but it will begin to introduce a separate set of criteria against which appeals can be judged.

However, even the courts do not bring a unity to the system of accountability. The law plays an important role in US zoning, because of the need to ensure that the constitution is respected in the decisions taken by local authorities, but most cases are heard by courts at state level, and legal interpretations varied widely according to Cullingworth. The Supreme Court is the "final arbiter", but cases very rarely reach this level. For Cullingworth, this is all further evidence of the fragmentation and lack of system in US zoning. It demonstrates, too, that although legality and constitutionality are key concepts that inform US zoning, the degree of accountability offered by a pattern of zoning ordinances is a good deal less watertight than the theory would lead us to suppose.

Accountability in Britain

In Britain, the question of discretionary power does not pose the same kind of threat to legal process that it clearly does in France or the USA, since the discretionary power is clearly accorded by law. That in consequence has led to the need to adjudicate on matters of policy – in other words, factors that a local authority may legally entertain in reaching a decision because they are "material considerations" – but where there is doubt as to which factor is paramount. The primary form of accountability is therefore not legal but administrative and is enshrined in the right of the applicant to appeal to central government against the decision of the local authority. The chosen form for hearing appeals has been in the first instance the public local inquiry, with an inspector appointed in a dual role of information gatherer, and in most circumstances now, of decision-maker. The public inquiry, one of a family of administrative tribunals, is a mechanism of some standing, introduced originally to deal with the problem of enclosures in the nineteenth century (Wraith & Lamb 1971). Already having proved its worth, it was grafted onto the planning system after 1947 and has proved in most circumstances robust enough to deal with the matters of policy upon which development control decisions rest. Local authorities are forced to justify their reasons for refusing development, and developers are able to argue why the material considerations do in fact support their proposals. The Tesco Meadowhead case also demonstrates how important inquiries have become as the forum in which objections can be heard.

There are, however, several significant weaknesses in the process of administrative accountability represented by public inquiries. The first is the difficulty of setting national policy and practices against local impact. The inquiries into the nuclear power station at Sizewell, or the development of the coalfield at Belvoir, showed how objectors to a proposal might take the local effect of a proposal as evidence of the weakness of a national policy, which had given rise to the need for development. One way around this particular problem was to use joint or linked inquiries to be able to balance the material considerations in strategic policy with those that related to specific sites (Couper & Barker 1981).

A second weakness that severely tested the inquiry system in the 1970s was the problem created if central government was not entirely open about the material upon which a decision was to be based. In the case of the Belvoir coalfield, for example, the Minister responsible later admitted that the inquiry took place in the light of two policy documents, apparently the outcome of agreements between the government, the National Coal Board and the National Union of Mineworkers (*Journal of Planning Environment Law* 1980). Even more threatening to the system of inquiries as a whole were the inquiries into major road proposals in the 1970s, which were hotly contested and in which objectors argued that the Department of Transport did not reveal the full extent of the information on which their case was based (Levin 1979). Although these inquiries were held under the Highways Act and therefore had nothing to do with development control and town and country planning, they made clear the preconditions for effective public inquiries. The inspector had to be impartial and independent of those who took the decisions or were involved in promoting the development. All the information on which the decision was based needed to be available to everyone. Where these preconditions are met, as they were at the Tesco Meadowhead inquiry, then everyone feels that there has been a fair hearing of the case and the account is squared.

However, there is, a third weakness of the system: it operates only if a local authority refuses to grant planning permission. If the local authority grants planning permission, there is not very much third parties can do to contest the decision once taken. Central government has power to determine any application that it cares to call in, but although the power in the Town and Country Planning Act is very widely drawn, it is seldom used. Most of the applications called in are those that will have been notified to the DoE because they represent departures from approved plans in force, although locally controversial applications may also be called in (Barker & Couper 1984). Third-party concerns are by no means fully met by this procedure. After the local authority has taken a decision, third parties have only two courses of action. One is to seek judicial review, but this can only address the question of whether the process by which the decision has been taken was legal. The other is to contest the decision before the courts, but this requires the aggrieved party to pass a stringent test of *locus standi*: that the complainant is directly and adversely affected by the decision taken. In practice this is difficult to prove to the satisfaction of the courts, and the action is very rarely taken (Alder 1979).

This particular weakness is a direct result of the nationalization of development rights in the British planning system. Having taken such a drastic step, Parliament had then to ensure that those deprived of the right to develop had nevertheless the right to contest the decision to refuse planning permission. Accountability in the appeals system was to be of the local planning authority to the private land-owner, not to the public at large. There was not at the outset the same pressure for third-party rights, because, in exercising control, the local planning authority would be acting in the public interest. The local authority was obliged to take local representations into account in reaching a decision, and informing neigh-bours of applications lodged so that they knew when they might make represen-tations became an increasingly important part of the British development control system. Neighbour notification became a formal requirement in Scotland in 1981, and was finally introduced to England and Wales in the Planning and Compen-sation Act 1992.

Compared with the French and US systems, the British system of development control offers remarkably few formal guarantees to third parties. Instead, there are one or two important procedural rights, chiefly the right to be heard at public inquiries and to object to planning applications before the decision is taken. Of these, the former is sanctioned more frequently by reference to the principles of natural justice than it is by statutory requirement. The latter offers no guarantee that the local planning authority will act on an objection made, and there is no requirement to justify the decision taken in the light of such an objection. Such redress as there is would have to be by judicial review, to determine whether the local planning authority had indeed taken the objection into account when reach-ing its decision.

Hong Kong

If Britain's rather fragile means of ensuring that local authorities account for their decisions works, it is because of the distance that exists between local authorities and central government, and the *de facto* independence that inspectors are able to establish from both. Hong Kong has had difficulty in trying to model a system of appeals on British administrative practice because there is no such separation. As the planning ordinance stands at the moment, applicants may seek a review of decisions taken by the Town Planning Board, by appealing to the Board itself. If that review does not satisfy the appellant, there is a further possibility of appeal to the Governor-in-Council, the territory's highest governing authority. There is, however no automatic right to be heard by the Governor-in-Council, and the procedures are described as cumbersome. In all, this system hardly guarantees that the government will be held to account for its decision, or that objections will not simply be swept aside. The proposals in the Comprehensive Review were for a separate Appeal Board to which appeals would be made, and whose members would not include anyone involved in taking the original decision (Hong Kong 1991). This will do something to alleviate the problem, but the Appeal Board is likely to consist of the same category of people as the Town Planning Board and may still not remove the potential for collusion.

Looked at from another point of view, the problem in Hong Kong is not as acute as it might be in Britain, because of the extent to which developers have development rights, without the need to apply for planning permission at all. This is to overlook the fact that it is with contentious issues – the areas where there are discretionary freedoms – that the question of accountability arises. The small but intractable number of cases that are exceptions in some way to the general rule are the ones that test the system, in any country.

Ensuring accountability: some conclusions

All the systems of development control we have looked at sooner or later permit or encourage discretionary action. Calling decision-makers to account for the powers they exercise is a necessary part of those systems. Two observations must be made, however, about accountability. The first is that all the systems use several sorts of accounting mechanism: none rely solely on one means of keeping decision-makers in line. The second is that those systems are far from being fully effective. In relation to the first point, for those systems of control in which legality is paramount, there are nevertheless alternatives to the courts for ensuring accountability, in the form of administrative procedures. In France, the prefect vets all decisions taken, albeit on the grounds of legality, but clearly exercises considerable discretion about how to act when a decision appears to be illegal. In the USA, the Board of Appeal forms the primary means of redress, and these Boards may introduce an independent set of criteria for taking decisions. The existence of these administrative mechanisms is a reflection both of the cumbersome nature of legal procedures, and, perhaps too, of the inappropriateness of legal criteria on their own for planning control decisions. In the quite different context of Britain, accountability before Parliament, or of individual decision-makers before the courts, could never be adequate to deal with the increasingly complex questions of planning policy that inform control decisions. Hence, the appeal system and public inquiries have a key role in ensuring that the system is more fully accountable.

In considering the effectiveness of systems of accountability, several issues arise. The distinction between systems that confer substantive rights is one such issue. The presence of substantive rights such as those conferred by the administrative law tradition is evidently not a guarantee of satisfaction on the part of

141

those who seek redress. The French case studies reveal how those rights can be effectively eroded by discretionary action, whether, as in the Transports Griset case, the discretion is formalized, or whether, as in Le Soleil Levant, it is entirely officer discretion. What infuriated the residents of Le Pellet, however, was not only the nature of the Griset extension, but the fact that they could not *see* how the decision was being justified. Much the same feeling seems to have been present in the Meadowhead case. While the application was being processed, residents believed a deal was being stitched up between Tesco and the City Council, which excluded their point of view. But the difference between Meadowhead and Le Pellet lay in the public inquiry that gave Meadowhead residents the chance of a fair hearing, which Le Pellet residents felt they had been denied.

Transparency in the procedures by which decisions are accounted for is clearly of some significance. A further issue is the independence of the body to which the decisions are referred. The British inquiry system was threatened with collapse when there appeared to be collusion between central government departments and inspectors. The risk of collusion between different arms of the French administration also appears to attenuate accountability. Procedures in Hong Kong seem designed for a distance between structures that cannot exist in a territory so limited in its size. However, the existence of an independent authority is not itself a guarantee that a satisfactory accounting mechanism is in place. The body of referral may just be another discretionary actor using its own system of criteria to review others' decisions. Thus, US Boards of Appeal, for example, further fragment the system of zoning ordinances.

Ensuring that decision-makers do account for their decisions is thus not a simple process. The mechanisms adopted are a direct reflection of the administrative and legal cultures of the countries that produce them. How far, then, do they really ensure accountability and thereby protect the rights of users of the system? What balance of substantive and procedural rights are necessary? And how well do they deal with the nature of land-use planning and control?

CHAPTER 8
Conclusion

The starting point for the discussion of the development control systems in Britain and France was the activities of Henri IV and Charles I in promoting an ideal of city form in the piazzas of Covent Garden and the Place Royale. These two initiatives exemplified the general principle that the desire to control development stems from a wish to be certain that in future the city will conform to perceptions of good order of whatever kind. Indeed, even if some systems of development control lay a heavier premium on certainty than others, all control activities tend in that direction and various mechanisms have been used to achieve the desired ends. These include direct intervention by the controlling authority, the use of dimensional norms for buildings and, more recently, the preparation of plans to which individual control decisions could be referred. Certainty has become an issue, not simply for the controlling authority, with its vision of the perfect city towards which the control activity works, but for anyone with a stake in the development process.

Much of the material in this book suggests that this search for certainty is fraught with complications. Logically, absolute certainty about future development is an impossibility and in effect much of the work of development control systems is about grappling with future uncertainty. The problem is all too frequently knowing where the limits of accurate prediction really lie. Having said that, two general points emerge from the discussion of the development control systems and of the case studies. The first is that the search for certainty may in the end be paradoxically self-defeating. This is particularly in evidence in the increasing elaboration of the zoning mechanisms in the USA, which have led to a complexity that is so far from increasing certainty, that it militates against it. Although British local plans are entirely different from both US and French zoning plans, there is nevertheless good reason to enquire whether the new requirement to provide district-wide plans will in fact reduce the vagaries of British development control. The second is that greater certainty is by no means welcomed all the time by all those involved in the process. Time and again in the case studies we saw developers and public authorities alike chafing at the rigidity of pre-set limits whose intention it was to ensure future certainty, but which no longer appeared to fit the facts of the matter in hand. Whether or not the frustration with those limits was always justified, it nevertheless exemplified the need for development control systems to cope with future change and uncertainty, which is universal. To argue that uncertainty and the need for change are inevitable should not obscure the fact that least some of the time certainty, even if it is not absolute, is both desired and necessary. In Chapter 5 the distinction was made between certainty of outcome and certainty of process, and at times different actors will want to maximize both. Sometimes, therefore, unequivocal statements of what is acceptable and unacceptable may be necessary and will need to be adhered to. Equally important may be the need to know, not so much what the outcome of what a decision will be, but when and how the decision will be taken.

One kind of acknowledgement of the inevitability of future uncertainty is to ask that development control should be flexible in its operation. Those who seek flexibility take the view that control decisions should not be too constrained by rigid limits when common sense suggests that those limits are no longer realistic. As with attitudes to certainty, the desire for flexibility in development control springs from a variety of motives that are not necessarily admirable. Developers urge local authorities to be flexible in their approach because it is through negotiation that developers are able to maximize the profitability of their schemes, particularly by arguing a special case. Local authorities have also favoured flexibility as a means of obtaining ultimate power over decision-making. Limits too tightly defined in advance will mortgage future power to act. If flexibility may be used abusively, its presence in the vocabulary of development control is also a recognition that future uncertainty cannot wholly be spirited away by prior prescription. Yet if flexibility is advocated as the response to over-rigid formulation of the limits to development, too much flexibility also presents problems, particularly for the decision-maker. If the field of a decision is entirely without constraint, there appears to be a tendency to formulate rules to limit the options available. Flexibility is by no means an unalloyed blessing, even to its beneficiaries.

The discussion of flexibility does, moreover, take us into a discussion of the much more difficult question of discretionary power. The question is difficult because of the nature of the discretion involved, and the differences between the different actors' use of discretion and the means by which those actors justify their use of the power they exercise. Some uses of discretion seem to be more difficult than others, because there is no effective check on how the discretionary power is exercised. Thus, if there is to be flexibility in the development control process, implying the existence of discretionary power, there has within democratic systems of government to be a way of ensuring that those who have discretionary power account for its use. In practice, as we saw, the different systems of control all operate several different mechanisms for ensuring the accountability of decision-makers, which are variously judicial, administrative and political. Once again, however, it is important to distinguish between substantive accountability, which allows others to question the decisions taken by those with discretion to act, and procedural transparency, which ensures only the process by which a decision is reached is exposed to view. As we saw in Chapter 7, both are important. Those involved need to be able to see both the process by which a decision was taken and the manner in which it was taken and, in the event, influence both. Without those mechanisms for accountability, there is a real danger that the flexible response and the discretionary power become arbitrary.

From this rapid review of the three major themes of the book, the question arises as to whether it is possible to evaluate the British and French systems in terms of the certainty they create for the users of the systems, the freedom that they offer to respond to change and uncertainty, and the capacity for accountability that each possesses.

The British system emphasizes flexibility as a means of ensuring that appropriate development takes place as and when it is needed. Moreover, there is explicit recognition of the discretionary power needed to offer the desired level of flexible response. The explicit recognition of discretionary power granted to local authorities makes it easier in principle to ensure that the exercise of that power is duly accounted for. Three potential tools are available: politically at local elections; in terms of policy laid down both locally and nationally through the appeals system; and judicially when decisions are challenged on the grounds of their legality rather than in relation to policy. Of them, the appeals system, and in particular the local public inquiry used as a means for exploring the policy grounds of the decision, has shown considerable resilience and has been widely accepted as a fair and open means of reaching a decision. Yet the emphasis on discretionary freedom has had several serious adverse consequences, too. One is the failure to formulate policy, because there is no absolute need to do so; control of development can continue quite happily in the absence of declared policy, relying on the "other material considerations" clause of the Act to find a basis for an appropriate decision. It has resulted in, among other things, the incoherence and vacillations of policy on design both locally and nationally; it also has meant, until 1992, a poor coverage of the country by local plans. Another problem has been the way in which lack of certainty in outcome, which is an essential characteristic of a discretionary system, and the absence of rights to development have led to an undue emphasis being placed on the efficiency of the system and in particular on the question of delay. A third problem is that the appeals system only operates to provide rights for users of the system if the local authority has refused a planning application. Third parties have few rights to challenge a local authority's decision, should it be favourable to the development being considered.

The French system, with its emphasis on certainty, does not suffer from the same difficulties, either with regard to the basis on which a decision is taken, or to the question of third-party rights. Moreover, the *POS* provide a high level of detail, which goes a long way to vindicating the emphasis on certainty. Yet in spite of that, the French system seems often unable to deliver the certainty that is desired, as we have seen, to the consternation of the French themselves. The desire for flexibility that is articulated and accepted in the British system is present but largely covert in France. Much of the discretion exercised is low-order judgement, made about the applicability of a rule. However, some is a result of explicit options offered by the regulations themselves, and then give rise to another kind of problem.

The emphasis on certainty and on legal right is part of a decision that has created a legal means of redress for citizens against the activities of the state. The rights of third parties are as strong in France as they are weak in Britain. The difficulty with the use of the legal system as the main means of redress is that the criterion by which decisions are judged is primarily whether they are legal, rather than whether they are opportune. This would seem to be particularly problematic where there is explicit discretionary power offered by the regulations themselves, whether locally produced in the *POS* or nationally in the *Code de l'urbanisme*. In time the administration courts may become adapted to dealing with distinctions between policy as the number of such decisions increases, but the administrative judge is not self evidently the best placed to make such decisions. In any case the evidence of the case studies and of the system as a whole is that such policy debate is actually conducted in the largely unexposed dealings between technical service personnel, prefects and mayors, particularly through the prefects' exercise of the *contrôle de légalité*. This, as the case of Le Soleil Levant suggested, involved two discretionary actors, both acceptable for the law, but whose decisions and counter-decisions are rarely accessible, other than as accepted fact.

The easy conclusion to draw from this evaluation of the British and French systems is that, if the British system became a little more like the French and the French like the British, then each would have the best of both worlds. We have seen how Wakeford wondered whether the British system was not moving towards a more regulatory approach, while the US system was becoming more discretionary, and more recently others have suggested that the passing of the Planning and Compensation Act, and the renewed emphasis on development plans, was bringing the British system more closely in line with the systems of its other European partners. Such an argument is, in all but the most general terms, fallacious. In Chapter 4, the argument was advanced that the distinctive character of zoning systems, derived from an understanding of the state and the role of law, was substantially different from that in Britain. So deeply ingrained is this kind of understanding and the fact that it goes far beyond the question of land-use control means that a system cannot become "more regulatory" or "more discretionary" without severely straining the nature of government as a whole. The British and French apparatus of government have perceived the objectives of controlling land-use activity and development, and have grafted them into patterns of administration in very different ways. The development control systems have been able to deliver substantially different successes, as well as revealing some considerable difficulties. The starting point for any evaluation must be the successes and failures, both as seen from within and as visible from outside.

Absolute certainty – providing a rule for every circumstance – is self-evidently an impossibility, because it is never possible to foresee every circumstance. The lesson of the case studies is that there is always a push to create leeway in decision-making, whether this is needed to respond to the unforeseeable or whether it is a manoeuvre to retain ultimate control over decisions. Faced with this inevitability, there appear to be two responses. One is the move towards increasing elaboration, as has happened in both France and the USA. The other is to argue for a return to elemental simplicity, to strip the regulations of the over-elaboration in order to regain clarity and by that means a new certainty. Although both approaches are understandable from within the context that produced them, neither is finally satisfying. The problem of over-elaboration has been discussed above. The retreat from what Bouyssou (1986) has referred to as the "Byzantine complexity" of planning regulations as they have developed in France does not seem to provide a complete answer either. The trouble about urging a greater simplicity by resorting to a few clear rules is that to do so does not reflect the complexity of land-use allocation problems or a desire to impose control. The simple rules might only serve as a mask for an ever-greater array of covert discretionary actions than exist at present.

If complete certainty is an unobtainable goal, so too, is complete flexibility. No decision is made entirely in the light of circumstances that obtain at the moment of making it, because, even if made by tossing a coin, there is reference to some kind of pre-established criterion. Complete open-endedness is in any case somewhat threatening. Development control systems abhor a vacuum and will create their own rules, even if those rules are not fully articulated, to ease the tension that making decisions creates. Moreover, complete flexibility, even if it were possible, does not respond to the legitimate need of all actors in the process to be sure at least about some aspects of future development. Where does the balance lie?

There are essentially two issues at stake. The first was touched upon in Chapter 5 and it concerns the way in which the policy on which decisions are based is expressed. Rules that denote fixed limits are without question easy to apply and in theory brook no argument. In practice, they all too often become the baseline for bargaining and negotiation, which fundamentally weakens their impact. That they are so used arises from the fact that many fixed rules do not accurately reflect the complexity of the urban environment and the goals of the planning system. Although at times some constraints must be converted into fixed limits because the objectives are clear – such was the case at Vénissieux – many objectives can be met by a variety of means because they do not easily translate in this way. Objectives may also interact such that blind observance of a particular constraint may not be useful. Performance criteria may in many cases be a more helpful way of expressing the underlying policy objectives that control is expected to implement.

The second important issue connected with flexibility and certainty has to do with making the areas of choice clear from the outset. Recognition of where discretionary action is possible and indeed necessary begins to make any system of development control more transparent. It helps to distinguish between those things that need to be certain and those when areas of doubt and uncertainty exist. In so doing it gives a measure of security to all the users of the system and helps to define where the areas of argument, if any, will be. It ensures that the parameters of future development may become clearer.

As we have seen, both French regulations and British policy statements not infrequently already offer choices to decision-makers, as the case studies make clear. The Transports Griset case was just such an example and it proved profoundly unsatisfying to the residents of the Le Pellet. Two things were missing at Le Pellet that meant that the decision taken appeared to residents to be entirely arbitrary. One was the absence of the performance criteria against which the eventual decision could be judged. The other was in a sense more serious: the absence of any mechanism for allowing the decision to be evaluated in an open fashion. The basis for the judgement, that the impact of the extension would not make conditions worse, was never exposed. Nor was it fully clear who was actually responsible for the decision, even if formally the power rested with the mayor, because there was in this case a *POS* in force.

All of this again emphasizes that process is as important as content in development control. The frustrations of those affected by decisions of local authorities is considerably relieved if the procedures by which decisions are taken are transparent and if there are rights to be involved in the process. In France, Bourny (1986) and Prieur (1990) have advocated the development of the *enquête publique* (public inquiry) into a device that would be used for development control decisions, in addition to its current use for investigating the preparation of *POS*. This would entail a professionalization of the role of inspector on British lines and an increase in the independent status of inspectors. In Britain the proposal to extend the right to appeal against a decision to third parties is at least being discussed, and a former Chief Inspector has declared himself in favour (Crow 1995). It is important to note that this apparent exchange of its strength between the two systems is not a simplistic transfer of practice, in that each proposal is the development of existing procedures. Under Hostiou's proposal, France would not acquire a British system of inquiries, but an improved version of the *enquête publique* extended in scope to deal with development control decisions. Crow and others who have advocated the third-party right to appeal against local authorities' planning decisions have undoubtedly been influenced by the stark contrast between such rights in continental Europe and their absence in Britain, but Crow takes his immediate cue from Ireland, which has already demonstrated that, in a discretionary system, third-party rights need not be absent.

Finding the right way to express policy, creating a process that is transparent, and ensuring the discretionary action is properly accounted for, form a major part of the story. The actual methods used must of course be specific to the administrative and political framework in which the control system is located. It is important, however, that the needs, perceptions and attitudes of those who use the system are fully understood. We saw in Chapter 5 how equivocal attitudes to certainty are in practice and how different actors understood the need for certainty in very different ways. Attitudes are to some extent generated by the systems themselves. In France, the right to property, which includes rights to future development (be those rights never so circumscribed) generate expectations of the development control process that are absent in Britain. In contrast, British developers have developed a negotiating style that directly reflects the discretionary freedoms under British planning legislation. Equally, their concern for delay is in the end a reflection not of the time it takes to process applications but of the absence of any right to develop without a valid planning permission. As important as developers' attitudes is the recognition that people affected by development control decisions also have a need to be certain about the future application of policy and the ability to question decisions that are taken.

This discussion can be distilled into a series of basic points:

- Systems for controlling development need to recognize that absolute certainty is unobtainable, but should be able to define the limits of uncertainty.
- Entirely open-ended systems of control nevertheless depend on standards and criteria that may not be fully articulated. Unwritten rules and practices will be devised to lessen the difficulty of taking decisions.
- Negotiation and bargaining are an essential part of the development control process and will take place no matter how rigid the framework was within which the decisions are made. Development control systems need to ensure that the parameters of such negotiations are clear and the process not obscured.
- The presence of discretionary decision-making of whatever kind is inevitable in development control. Criteria for evaluating the use of discretionary power are essential.
- Both the basis on which decisions are taken and the process by which they are taken need to be reasonably accessible for users of the system.
- Mechanisms for ensuring the accountability of decision-making need to offer the possibility of debating the appropriateness of decisions.

The ways in which different development control systems reflect these points will of course be specific to the systems themselves. Nor will the satisfactory resolution of these points lead to a process of controlling development that is free from tension or controversy. However, there is another factor that has scarcely been touched on in this book, which will have a bearing on the effectiveness of development control in Britain and France. Both are currently undergoing a process of local government reform that in the longer term may greatly affect the capacity of public authorities to respond to the problems of regulating future urban development. The current reforms are part of a longstanding debate that has run in parallel to the debate on the nature of development control charted here. The impact of these reforms on the ability to prepare planning policy and to implement that policy through decisions taken on development proposals will be of great significance in the future. But that is already another story.

Glossary

bestemmingsplan   Local land use plan in the Netherlands

commune   The lowest unit of French local government.

communauté urbaine   Grouping of communes in nine of the major urban areas of France with responsibilities prescribed by law including forward planning. Introduced by legislation in 1966.

communauté de communes, communauté de villes   New forms of intercommunal grouping introduced by the Loi de l'Administration Territoriale de la République 1992.

contrôle de légalité   Control exercised by the prfect in France of decisions taken by units of local government to ensure that such decisions are legal.

DDE   Direction Départementale de l'Équipement: field service of the central government ministry responsible for planning in each of the 96 *départements* of metropolitan France.

département   Unit of French local government roughly equivalent to English counties in area.

Development Permission Area   In Hong Kong, areas, mainly in the rural parts of the New Territories, where consent is required for new development.

district   *In Britain*: Lowest unit of local government with responsibilities for plan-making and development control. *In France*: Grouping of communes with some responsibilities prescribed by law and a power to raise its own tax. Introduced by legislation in 1959.

Outline Zoning Plan   Hong Kong zoning plan specifying uses permitted as-of-right ("Column 1") and uses which the Town Planning Board has discretion to permit ("Column 2").

permis de construire   Permission to build: the authorization required under the *Code de l'urbanisme* before building work may proceed.

POS   *plan d'occupation des sols*: local land-use plan. A zoning plan with regulations usually produced to cover the area of a single commune. The plan is binding on all parties and contestable at law.

RNU   *règles nationales d'urbanisme*: national planning regulations. Regulations in the *code de l'urbanisme* to cover the grounds for determining *permis de construire* in communes without a *POS*.

SD   *schéma directeur d'aménagement de d'urbanisme*: strategic plan for development and planning. A plan usually prepared for a group of communes and in urban areas or areas of development pressure, it is binding only upon the administration.

uitbredingsplan   Town extension plan in the Netherlands replaced after 1962 by the *bestemmingsplan*.

ZAC   *zone d'aménagement concerté*: concerted development zone. Zones used to define areas where development is imminent or is to be promoted.

ZUP   *zone à urbaniser en priorité*: priority development zone. Zoning used to promote large areas for housing development. Replaced by *ZAC*.

References

Adler, M. & S. Asquith (eds) 1981. *Discretion and welfare*. London: Heinemann.

Agence d'urbanisme de la Communauté urbaine de Lyon 1982. *Plan d'occupation des sols secteur sud-ouest*. Lyon: The Agence.

— 1985. *Plan d'occupation des sols de Lyon*. Lyon: the Agence.

Alder, J. 1990. Planning agreements and planning powers. *Journal of Planning and Environment Law*, 880–89.

Alder, J. 1979. *Development control*. London: Sweet & Maxwell.

Ashworth, S. 1993. Plymouth and after (II). *Journal of Planning and Environment Law* (December), 1105–1110.

Association des Études Foncières (ed.) 1987. *La règle et l'urbanisme*. Paris: l'Association des Études Foncières.

Auby, J-B. 1987. La règle d'urbanisme entre stabilité et flexibilité. See Association des Études Foncières (1987: 233–46).

Babcock, R. F. 1966. *The zoning game*. Madison: University of Wisconsin Press.

Babcock, R. F. & C. L. Siemon 1990. *The zoning game revisited*. Cambridge, Mass.: Lincoln Institute of Land Policy.

Babelon, J-P. 1982. *Henri IV*. Paris: Fayard.

Barker, A. & M. Couper 1984. The art of quasi-judicial administration: the planning appeal and inquiry systems in England. *Urban Law and Policy* **6**, 363–476.

Barlow, M. 1940. *Report of the Royal Commission of the Distribution of Industrial Population* [Cmnd 6153]. London: HMSO.

Baron, T. 1980. Planning's biggest and least satisfied customer. *Proceedings of the Town and Country Planning Summer School*, 6–17 September, 34–40 [supplement to *The Planner*].

Bastié, J. 1964. *La croissance de la banlieue parisienne*. Paris: Presses Universitaires de France.

Bergel, J-L. 1973. *Les servitudes de lotissement à usage d'habitation*. Paris: Pichon et Durand-Auzias.

Besson, M. 1971. *Les lotissements*. Paris: Berger–Levrault.

Bonneville, M. 1979. *Villeurbanne*. Lyon: Presses Universitaires de Lyon.

Booth, P. 1980. Speculative housing and the land market in London 1660–1730: four case studies. *Town Planning Review* **51**, 379–98.

— 1983. Development control and design quality: conditions: a useful way to control design? *Town Planning Review* **54**, 265–84.

— 1987. Design control. In *Planning control: philosophies, prospects, practice*, M. L. Harrison & R. A. Mordey (eds), 121–40. London: Croom Helm.

— 1988. *Rural development control in France: agreements between state and commune in Rhône and Haute-Loire*. Working Paper TRP83, Department of Town and Regional Planning, University of Sheffield.

— 1989. How effective is zoning in the control of development? *Environment and Planning B* **16**, 401–415.

— 1991. From *commune* to *communauté urbaine*: the legacy of the Revolution in the planning of Lyon. In *1789: the long and the short of it*, D. Williams (ed.), 121–37. Sheffield: Sheffield Academic Press.

—1994. *The MARNU: an effective means for rural settlement planning in France?* Working Paper TRP 123, Department of Town and Regional Planning, University of Sheffield.

Booth, P. & M. Gibbs 1993. *Defending local amenity: the Tesco superstore proposal at Meadowhead, Sheffield*. Working Paper TRP120, Department of Town and Regional Planning, University of Sheffield.

Booth, P. & T. Stafford 1994. Revisions and modifications: the effect of change on French plans d'occupations des sols. *Environment and Planning B* **21**, 305–322.

Bordessoule, A. & P. Guillemin 1956. *Les collectivités locales et les problèmes de l'urbanisme et du logement*. Paris: Sirey.

Bourjol, M. 1975. *La réforme municipale, bilan et perspectives*. Paris: Berger–Levrault.

Bourny, R. 1986. Le nouveau commissaire enquêteur. In *Les nouvelles procédures d'enquête publique*, J-C. Hélin, R. Hostiou, Y. Jégouzo, J. Thomas (eds), 29–39. Paris: Economica.

Bouyssou, F. 1987. La règle d'urbanisme et les garanties des administrés. See Association des Études Foncières (1987: 321–5).

Bowhill, A. 1980. Planning conditions in consents 1 and 2. *Estates Gazette* **256**, 993–4, 1085–1088.

Boyer, M. C. 1983. *Dreaming the rational city*. Cambridge, Mass.: MIT Press.

Bradshaw, J. 1981. From discretion to rules: the experience of the family fund. See Adler & Asquith (1981: 135–47).

Brindley, T., G. Stoker, Y. Rydin 1989. *Remaking planning: the politics of urban change in the Thatcher years*. London: Unwin Hyman.

Bristow, M. R. 1984. *Land-use planning in Hong Kong: history, policies and procedures*. Hong Kong: Oxford University Press.

Brock, D. 1994. Negotiating planning agreements after Tesco. *Journal of Planning and Environment Law* (August), 697–702.

Brown, L. N. & J. S. Bell 1993. *French administrative law*, 4th edn. Oxford: Oxford University Press.

Bull, D. 1980. The anti-discretion movement in Britain: fact or phantom. *Journal of Social Welfare Law* **3**(March), 65–84.

Burnett, J. 1986. *A social history of housing*, 2nd edn. London: Methuen.

Cabinet Office 1985. *Lifting the burden* [White Paper: Cmnd 9571]. London: HMSO.

Chabanol, D. 1986. Le contentieux du nouveau droit de l'urbanisme. *Les Cahiers de l'Institut de l'Aménagement du Territoire et de l'Environnement de l'Université de Reims* **7/8**, 277–85.

Chapuisat, J. 1983. *Le droit de l'urbanisme*. Paris: Presses Universitaires de France.

Chartier, R. & H. Neveux 1981. La ville dominante et soumise. See Duby (1981), 16–285.

Cherry, G. 1974. *The evolution of British planning*. Leighton Buzzard, England: Leonard Hill.

Choay, F. 1983. Pensées sur la ville, arts de la ville. In *Histoire de la France urbaine*, vol. 4: *la ville de l'âge industriel et le cycle Haussmannien*, G. Duby (ed.), 157–271. Paris: Seuil.

Comby, J. 1989. L'impossible propriété absolue. In *Un droit inviolable et sacré: la propriété*, Association des Études Foncières (eds), 9–20. Paris: The Association.

Commissariat Général du Plan 1993. *Villes démocratie, solidarité: le pari d'une politique* [Rapport du groupe "villes"]. Paris: La Documentation Française.

Conseil d'État 1992. *L'urbanisme: pour un droit plus efficace*. Paris: La Documentation Française.

Couper, M. & A. Barker 1981. Joint and linked inquiries: the superstore experience. *Journal of Planning and Environment Law*, 631–55.

Cox, A. 1984. *Adversary land and politics*. Cambridge: Cambridge University Press.

Crow, S. 1995. Third party appeals: will they work? Do we want them? *Journal of Planning and Environment Law*, 376–87.

Cullingworth, J. B. 1975. *Environmental planning 1939–1969*, vol. 1: *reconstruction and land use planning 1939–1947*. London: HMSO.

—1980. *Environmental planning 1939–1969*, vol. 4: *land values, compensation and betterment*. London: HMSO.

—1993. *The political culture of planning: American land-use planning in a comparative perspective*. New York: Routledge.

Danna, P-P. & J-D. Driard 1991. L'application anticipée des révisions de POS. *Études Foncières* **53**, 15–21.

Davey, S. & F. C. Minshull 1923. *The law and practice of town planning*. London: Butterworth.

Davies, H. W. E., D. Edwards, A. R. Rowley 1986. The relationship between development plans, development control and appeals. *The Planner* **72**(10), 11–15.

Davies, H. W. E. 1988. Control of development in the Netherlands. *Town Planning Review* **59**, 207–225.

Davies, H. W. E. 1980. The relevance of development control. *Town Planning Review* **51**, 5–17.

Davis, K. C. 1971. *Discretionary justice*. Urbana: University of Illinois Press.

Delrue, M. 1993. L'intercommunalité un an après la loi Joxe. *Le Moniteur des Travaux Publics* (4660), 38–40.

Department of Employment 1985. *Building businesses . . . not barriers*. [White Paper: Cmnd 9794]. London: HMSO.

DoE [Department of Environment] 1973. *Streamlining the planning machine* [Circular 142/73]. London: HMSO.

—1975. *Review of the development control system: final report by Mr George Dobry QC* [Circular 113/75]. London: HMSO.

—1980. *Development control: policy and practice* [Circular 22/80]. London: HMSO.

—1983. *Town and Country Planning Act 1971: Planning gain* [Circular 22/83]. London: HMSO.

—1984a. *Land for housing* [Circular 15/84]. London: HMSO.

—1984b. *Industrial development* [Circular 16/84]. London: HMSO.

—1985. *Development and employment* [Circular 14/85]. London: HMSO.

—1986. *The future of development plans* [consultation paper]. London: The Department.

—1988. *General policy and principles* [PPG1]. London: HMSO.

—1989. *The future of development plans* [White Paper: Cmnd 569]. London: HMSO.

—1991. *Sports and recreation* [PPG17] London: HMSO.

—1992. General policy and principles [PPG1 revised]. London: HMSO.

Department of Trade and Industry 1988. *Releasing enterprise* [White Paper: Cmnd 512]. London: HMSO.

Dequéant, J. 1994. Coopération oui! Fusion non! *Le Moniteur des Travaux Publics* (4711), 440.

Dobry, G. 1974. *Control of demolition*. London: HMSO.

—1975. *Review of the development control system: final report*. London: HMSO.

Duby, G. (ed.) 1981. *Histoire de la France urbaine*, vol. 3: *la ville classique de la Renaissance aux Révolutions*. Paris: Seuil.

Dupuy, F. & J-C. Thoenig 1985. *L'administration en miettes*. Paris: Fayard.

Dworkin, R. 1977. *Taking rights seriously*. London: Duckworth.

155

Dyson, K. H. F. 1980. *The state tradition in Western Europe*. Oxford: Martin Robertson.

Essex County Council 1973. *A design guide for residential areas*. Chelmsford: Essex County Council.

Evans, D. M. E. 1971. Some legal aspects of urbanization in Hong Kong. In *Asian urbanization: a Hong Kong casebook*, D. J. Dwyer (ed.) 20–32. Hong Kong: Hong Kong University Press.

Evenson, N. 1979. *Paris: a century of change, 1878–1978*. New Haven, Connecticut: Yale University Press.

Fair, J. 1994. Pressure groups push up the cost of UDPs. *Planning Week* **2**(14), 8.

Flockton, C. H. 1983. French local government reform and urban planning. *Local Government Studies* **12**(September–October), 65–77.

François, L. 1976. *Les institutions de la France*. Paris: Hachette.

Gaudin, J-P. 1985. *L'avenir en plan: technique et politique dans le prévision urbaine 1900–1930*. Seyssel: Champ Vallon.

Gilbert, A. 1993. Plymouth and after (I). *Journal of Planning and Environment Law* (December), 1099–104.

Girouard, M. 1985. *Cities and people*. New Haven, Connecticut: Yale University Press.

Glasson, B. & P. Booth 1992. Negotiation and delay in the development control process. *Town Planning Review* **63**, 63–8.

Gontcharoff, G. & S. Milano 1985. *La décentralisation 1: nouveaux pouvoirs nouveaux enjeux*. Paris: Syros.

Gourevitch, P. A. 1980. *Paris and the provinces: politics of local government reform in France*. Berkeley: University of California Press.

Grant, M. (ed.) 1991. *Encyclopaedia of planning law and practice*, July, Part A: *Recent developments* [monthly bulletin]. London: Sweet & Maxwell.

Grant, M. 1991. Recent developments. *Encyclopaedia of Planning Law and Practice*. Monthly Bulletin, July, 1–7.

Grant, M. (ed.) 1992. *Encyclopaedia of planning law and practice*. London: Sweet & Maxwell.

Grimley, J. R. Eve & Thames Polytechnic 1922. *The use of planning agreements* [DoE research report]. London: HMSO.

Grist, B. 1995. Development control in the Republic of Ireland: comparative aspects. Conference on "Our planning future", Oxford Brookes University, 29–31 March.

Guichard, O. 1976. *Vivre ensemble*. Paris: La Documentation Française.

Haar, C. M. 1989. Reflections on *Euclid: social contract and private purpose*. See Haar & Kayden (1989: 333–54).

Haar, C. M. & J. R. Kayden (eds) 1989a. *Zoning and the American dream: promises still to keep*. Chicago: Planners Press.

Haar, C. M. & J. S. Kayden 1989b. Foreword: zoning at sixty – a time for anniversary reckonings. See Haar & Kayden (1989) ix–xi.

Hall, P. 1973. *The containment of urban England* [2 volumes]. London: Allen & Unwin.

Ham, C. & M. Hill 1984. *The policy process in the modern capitalist state*. Brighton, Sussex: Wheatsheaf.

Hampton, W. 1987. *Local government and urban politics*. Harlow, England: Longman.

Harlow, C. & R. Rawlings 1984. *Law and administration*. London: Weidenfeld & Nicolson.

Harper, R. H. 1985. *Victorian building regulations 1840–1914*. London: Mansell.

Harris, J. 1989. *Inigo Jones: universal man*. In *Inigo Jones: complete architectural draw-*

ings, J. Harris & A. Higgott (eds) 13–19. New York: Philip Wilson.

Harrison, M. 1975. Dobry and social policy. *The Planner* **61**, 236–7.

Haussmann, G-E. 1979. *Mémoires du Baron Haussmann: grands travaux de Paris* [facsimile of 3rd edn, 1893 tome I]. Paris: Guy Durier.

Heidenheimer, A. 1986. Politics, policy and policey as concepts in English and continental language: an attempt to explain divergences. *The Review of Politics* **48**, 3–30.

Hocreitère, P. 1991. La volatilité de la règle d'urbanisme. In *Sécurité et transparence des marchés immobiliers*, Association des Études Foncières (eds), 93–106. Paris: l'Association des Études Foncières.

Hong Kong Planning Environment and Lands Branch 1991. *Comprehensive review of the Town Planning Ordinance*. Hong Kong: Government Secretariat.

House of Commons 1986. *Planning appeals, call-in and major public inquiries* [Environment Committee Session 1985-6, 5th Report]. London: HMSO.

— 1977. *Planning procedures* [Expenditure Committee Session 1976-77, 8th Report; 3 volumes]. London: HMSO.

Howells, C. 1983. Relative discretion and the evolution of transport policy: a case study. In *Evaluating urban planning efforts*, I. Masser (ed.), 133–54. Aldershot: Gower.

Humber, R. 1990. Prospects and problems for private housebuilders. *Proceedings of the Town & Country Planning Summer School*, 23 February, 15–19.

Jégouzo, Y. & Y. Pittard 1980. *Le droit de l'urbanisme*. Paris: Masson.

Journal of Planning and Environment Law 1978. Current topics: the General Development Order – the amendments withdrawn. (January), 2–4.

— 1980. Current topics: planning inquiries – the new dimension. (November), 711–12.

Jowell, J. 1973. The legal control of administrative discretion. *Public Law*, 178–219.

Jowell, J. & M. Grant 1983. A critical look at planning gain. *Local Government Review* **147**(18 June), 491–3.

Keeble, L. 1964. *Principles and practice of town and country planning*, 3rd edn. London: Estates Gazette.

— 1983. *Town planning made plain*. London: Construction Press.

Knowles, C. C. & P. H. Pitt 1972. *The history of building regulation in London 1189–1972*. London: Architectural Press.

Labetoulle, D. 1982. *Le permis de construire*. Paris: Presses Universitaires de France.

Lagroye, J. & V. Wright (eds) 1979. *Local government in Britain and France: problems and prospects*. London: Allen & Unwin.

Le Moniteur des Travaux Publics 1985. Un bilan du contrôle de légalité des actes des collectivités locales. **50**(13 December), 63–4.

Le Roy Ladurie, E. 1981. Baroque et lumières. See Duby (1981: 288–535).

Legendre, P. 1964. *Histoire de l'administration de 1750 à nos jours*. Paris: Presses Universitaires de France.

Levin, P. H. 1979. Highway inquiries: a study in governmental responsiveness. *Public Administration* **57**, 21–49.

Logan, T. H. 1976. The Americanization of German zoning. In *Journal of the American Institute of Planners* **42**, 377–85.

Loughlin, M. 1982. 'Planning gain': another viewpoint. *Journal of Planning and Environment Law*, 352–8.

Loughlin, M. 1985. Administrative law, local government and the courts. In *Half a century of municipal decline, 1935-1995*, M. Loughlin, M. D. Gelfand, K. Young (eds), 121–43. London: Allen & Unwin.

Machin, H. 1979. *Traditional patterns of French local government.* See Lagroye & Wright (1979: 28–41).

Mariani, R. (ed.) 1990. *Tony Garnier: une cité industrielle.* New York: Rizzoli.

Martin, S. & G. Novarina 1987. *La pratique administrative et technicienne.* See Association des Études Foncières (1987: 326–32).

Maurice, R. 1976. *Le syndicat des communes.* Paris: Masson.

McAuslan, J. P. W. B. 1975. *Land, law and planning.* London: Weidenfeld & Nicolson.

— 1980. *The ideologies of planning law.* Oxford: Pergamon.

McBride, D. 1979. Planning delays and development control – a proposal for reform. *Urban Law and Policy* **2**, 47–64.

Minett, J. 1974. The Housing, Town Planning etc. Act 1909. *Planner* **60**, 676–80.

Ministère de l'Équipement, du Logement, des Transports et de la Mer 1991. Direction de l'Architecture et de l'Urbanisme. Unpublished statistics on *POS.*

Ministère de l'Équipement, du Logement, de l'Aménagement du Territoire et des Transports 1987. *Application à partir du 1er octobre de la règle dite de constructibilité limitée instituée par l'article L111-1-2a du code de l'urbanisme* [Circulaire du 24 septembre]. Paris: the Ministry.

Ministère de l'Urbanisme, du Logement, des Transports 1985. *Recueil des informations statistiques sur l'urbanisme.* Paris: the Ministry.

Ministère de l'Urbanisme, du Logement et des Transports & Ministère de l'Intérieur 1984. *Le contrôle de légalité des documents d'urbanisme décentralisés* [Circulaire du 2 Octobre]. Paris: the Ministries.

Ministry of Health 1919. *Housing Manual.* London: HMSO.

— 1933. Circular 1305. *Town and Country Planning Act.* London: HMSO.

Ministry of Housing and Local Government 1967. *Management study on development control.* London: HMSO.

Moor, N. & R. Langton 1978. *Planning for new homes.* London: N. Moor.

Moseley, H. 1986. Development control in New York City *Planner* **72**(12) 14–18.

Noble, D. 1981. From rules to discretion: the Housing Corporation. See Adler & Asquith (1981: 171–84).

Olsen, D. J. 1986. *The city as a work of art.* New Haven: Yale University Press.

Périnet-Marquet, H. 1986. Le contrôle de légalité en matière d'urbanisme. *Les Cahiers de l'Institut de l'Aménagement du Territoire et de l'Environnement de l'Université de Reims* **7/8**, 265–75.

Piron, O. 1994. 1943–1993: un anniversaire oublié. *Études Foncières* **62**, 34–6.

The Planner 1989a. Green light for Foxley Wood. **75**(12), 1, 3.

— 1989b. Final flurry on Foxley Wood. **75**(24), 7.

— 1989c. Howard firm on green belt. **75**(26), 8.

Planning 1980. AMA criticises circular with builders in defence. **383**(29 August), 1, 12.

— 1986. Use class reform plans get diluted. **673**(20 June), 1.

Planning Advisory Group 1965. *The future of development plans.* London: HMSO.

Planning Week 1995. RIBA: no aesthetic control for planning applications. **3**(24), 4.

Prats, Y., Y. Pittard, B. Touret 1979. *La dérogation d'urbanisme: le droit et la pratique.* Paris: Éditions du Champ Urbain.

Priet, F. 1992. La décentralisation de l'urbanisme – bilan et perspectives. In *Annuaire des collectivités locales*, G. Gilbert (ed.), 87–107. Paris: Librairies Techniques.

Prieur, M. 1990. *Les enquêtes publiques: quel avenir?* Paris: La Documentation Française.

Property Advisory Group 1982. *Planning gain.* London: HMSO.

— 1985. *Town and Country Planning (Use Classes) Order.* London: HMSO.

Punter, J. V. 1986. A history of aesthetic control, Part 1. *Town Planning Review* **57**, 351–81.

—1987. A history of aesthetic control, Part 2. *Town Planning Review* **58**, 20–62.

Purdue, M. 1994. The impact of Section 54A. *Journal of Planning and Environment Law*, 399–407.

Rabin, Y. 1989. Expulsive zoning: the inequitable legacy of *Euclid*. See Haar & Kayden (1989) 101–22.

Rhodes, R. A. W. 1980. Some myths in central–local relations. *Town Planning Review* **51**, 270–85.

—1986. "Power dependence": theories of central–local relationships. In *New research in central–local relations*, M. J. Goldsmith (ed.), 1–33. Aldershot: Gower.

Richard, P. & M. Cotten 1986. *Le communes françaises d'aujourd'hui*, 2nd edn. Paris: Presses Universitaires de France.

Richards, P. G. 1983. *The local government system*. London: Allen & Unwin.

Rickard, P. 1989. *A history of the French language*, 2nd edn. London: Unwin Hyman.

Rivais, R. 1994. Le groupement des communes est un succès. *Le Monde* [Heures Locales], 23–4 January, I, IV.

Roncayolo, M. 1983. La production de la ville. In *Histoire de la France urbaine*, vol. 4: *la ville de l'âge industriel et le cycle haussmannien*, G. Duby (ed.), 77–155. Paris: Seuil.

Rose, J. G. 1969. *Legal foundations of land-use planning*. Rutgers: The State University of New Jersey Press.

Scott, M. 1969. *American city planning since 1890*. Berkeley: University of California Press.

Sheppard, F. W. H. (ed.) 1970. *The parish of St Paul, Covent Garden* [Survey of London, vol. 36]. London: Athlone.

Slough Estates 1979. *Industrial investment: a case study in factory building*. Slough, Bucks: Slough Estates.

Smith, G. 1981. Discretionary decision-making in social work. See Adler & Asquith (1981), 47–68.

Sorbets, C. 1979. The control of development in France. See Lagroye & Wright (1979), 150–164.

Summerson, J. 1953. *Architecture in Britain 1530–1830*. London: Penguin.

—1966. *Inigo Jones*. London: Penguin.

—1978. *Georgian London*, 3rd edn. London: Barrie & Jenkins.

Sutcliffe, A. R. 1981. *Towards the planned city: Germany, Britain, the United States and France 1780–1914*. Oxford: Basil Blackwell.

Sutcliffe, A. R. 1970. *The autumn of central Paris*. London: Edward Arnold.

Tanguy, Y. 1979. *Le règlement des conflits en matière d'urbanisme*. Paris: Librairie générale de Droit et de Jurisprudence.

Thoenig, J-C. 1979. Local government institutions and the contemporary evolution of French society. See Lagroye & Wright (1979), 74–104.

Thomas, D., J. Minett, S. Hopkins, S. Hamnett, A. Faludi, D. Barrell 1983. *Flexibility and commitment in planning: a comparative study of local planning and development control in the Netherlands and England*. The Hague: Martinus Nijhoff.

Thorne, R. 1980. *Covent Garden market, its history and restoration*. London: Architectural Press.

Thornley, A. 1991. *Urban planning under Thatcherism: the challenge of the market*. London: Routledge.

Trintignac, A. 1964. *Aménager l'héxagone*. Paris: Centurion.

159

Underwood, J. 1980. Development control: a case study of discretion in action. In *Policy and action*, S. Barrett & C. Fudge (eds), 143–62. London: Methuen.

Uthwatt, A. A. 1941. *Expert Committee on Compensation and Betterment: interim report* [Cmnd 6291]. London: HMSO.

— 1942. *Expert Committee on Compensation and Betterment: final report* [Cmnd 6386]. London: HMSO.

Van Gunsteren, H. R. 1976. *The quest for control*. London: John Wiley.

Wakeford, R. 1990. *American development control: parallels and paradoxes from an English perspective*. London: HMSO.

Ward, S. 1974. The Town and Country Planning Act 1932. *The Planner* **60**, 685–9.

Weil, P. 1965. Strengths and weaknesses of French administrative law. *Cambridge Law Journal* **24**, 242–59.

Winock, M. 1989. *1789: l'année sans pareille*. Paris: Olivier Orban.

Wohl, A. S. 1977. *The eternal slum: housing and social policy in Victorian London*. London: Edward Arnold.

Woodford, G., K. Williams, N. Hill 1976. *The value of standards for the external residential environment*. London: DOE.

Wraith, R. E. & G. B. Lamb 1971. *Public inquiries as an instrument of government*. London: Allen & Unwin.

Yeh, A. G. O. 1994. Land leasing and urban form in Hong Kong. Paper presented at International Planning History Group Conference, Hong Kong.

Index